SATIRIC ART OF EVELYN WAUGH B
PR 6045 A97Z62

D0518174

Date Due

JAN 3 '61			
NO 21 '69			
JA 23 '70			
NO 16 '79			
NO 26 '79			
DE 7 '79			
JE 16 '82			
DE 10 '00			
MR 10 '10			

PR
6045
A97Z62

RIVERS[...]TY COLLEGE
LIBRARY
Riverside, California

bd PRINTED IN U.S.A.

THE SATIRIC ART OF EVELYN WAUGH

The Satiric Art of Evelyn Waugh

By

James F. Carens

1966
UNIVERSITY OF WASHINGTON PRESS
Seattle and London

Riverside City College Library
Riverside, California

PR6045.A97 Z62 1966
Carens, James F. (James Francis), 1927-
The satiric art of Evelyn Waugh,

Little, Brown and Company, publishers, has granted permission to reprint passages from the following books by Evelyn Waugh: *Decline and Fall,* copyright 1928, 1929, by Evelyn Waugh; *Vile Bodies,* copyright 1930 by Evelyn Waugh; *Black Mischief,* copyright 1932 by Evelyn Waugh; *A Handful of Dust,* copyright 1934 by Evelyn Waugh; *Scoop,* copyright 1937, 1938, by Evelyn Waugh; *Put Out More Flags,* copyright 1942 by Evelyn Waugh; *Brideshead Revisited,* copyright 1944, 1945, by Evelyn Waugh; *Scott-King's Modern Europe,* copyright 1947 by Evelyn Waugh; *Helena,* copyright 1950 by Evelyn Waugh; *Men at Arms,* copyright 1952 by Evelyn Waugh; *Officers and Gentlemen,* copyright 1955 by Evelyn Waugh; *The Ordeal of Gilbert Pinfold,* copyright 1957 by Evelyn Waugh; *The End of the Battle* (English title: *Unconditional Surrender),* copyright 1960 by Evelyn Waugh.

Copyright © 1966 by the University of Washington Press
Library of Congress Catalog Card Number 66-13540
Printed in the United States of America

Preface

EVELYN Waugh's career as a satirical novelist began in 1928 with the appearance of an ebullient and outrageous work, *Decline and Fall.* In that same year, the twenty-five-year-old writer also published a perceptive but not quite sympathetic biography of Dante Gabriel Rossetti. Since absolutely nothing seems to shock the author of *Decline and Fall,* it is odd to read *Rossetti* and to find its author distinctly offended by the excesses of the Pre-Raphaelite painter. But the truth of the matter is, the total detachment of *Decline and Fall* was a satiric mask. Waugh assumed that same mask in a second satire, *Vile Bodies* (1930), a work that further explored the follies of English society in the 1920's. Yet if detachment was Evelyn Waugh's satiric pose, in his life there was commitment, for, in the year of *Vile Bodies,* "on firm intellectual conviction but with little emotion," he was converted to Roman Catholicism.[1]

Even before his conversion, Waugh had embarked upon a way of life that was to prove as important to his artistic development as his religion. "From 1928 to 1937," Evelyn Waugh has written, "I had no fixed home and no possessions which would not conveniently go on a porter's barrow."[2] For nearly a decade, he traveled "continuously," producing a series of travel books and novels based on his journeys.

Labels (1930), a delightful recounting of a voyage around the Mediterranean, was the best of the travel books. Rereading the entire group in 1945, Waugh noticed that each book had a "distinct and slightly grimmer air, as, year by year, the shades of the prison house closed."[3] *Remote People* (1931) ridicules the coronation of Haile Selassie as emperor of Ethiopia and describes a nightmare journey through East Africa, which—excepting the Arab city of Harar, the Aden protectorate, and the English colony of Kenya—Waugh seems to have despised. *Ninety-Two Days* (1934), his least interesting book, recounts a journey in British Guiana and Brazil and is mostly concerned with the difficulties of travel. *Waugh in Abyssinia* (1936) marks his return to Ethiopia as a war correspondent, to report the Italian invasion of 1935; it is a work imbued with unmitigated contempt for the Ethiopians and Haile Selassie and with the highest admiration and respect for Mussolini's civilizing impulses. *Robbery Under Law* (1939) reveals even more fully Waugh's political position; it is not, properly speaking, an account of travels at all, but an attack on Mexican expropriation of British oil, a biased history of American intervention in the area, and an examination of the consequences of religious persecution in that violent land. Waugh chose to reprint nothing from *Robbery Under Law* in *When the Going Was Good,* a selection from the travel books published in 1946.

These travels also inspired a series of distinguished novels. *Black Mischief* (1932), as timely now as it was thirty years ago, is a burlesque of the attempted modernization of an African kingdom called Azania, which draws upon the first Ethiopian visit. *Scoop* (1938) draws upon the second and freely transforms the Italian intervention in Ethiopia into a political spoof. Newspapers, Africans, and Communists are the butts of most of the satire. *A Handful of Dust* (1934), an account of the corrosive effects of upper-class adultery, returned Waugh to England; but the concluding passage of the novel, Tony Last's agony in the Brazilian jungle, converts the tedium of *Ninety-Two Days* into horror and brilliant irony.

Although his political enthusiasms had led him to express sympathy with Mussolini in 1935 and Franco in 1938, when Evelyn Waugh's nation was threatened by the German dictator in 1939, he sprang to her defense, and, at the age of thirty-six, accepted a temporary commission in the Royal Marines. After Dunkirk, he was among the first to volunteer for commando work. In 1942 he transferred to the Royal Horse Guards with the rank of captain. Having seen action in North Africa and on Crete (where, according to Eric Linklater, he distinguished himself by courage in battle), he joined the British Military Mission to Yugoslavia.[4] After breaking his foot in a parachute jump made on this mission, he returned "by devious ways" to civilian life,[5] and to the publication of *Brideshead Revisited* (1945). *Brideshead* gave fuller expression to the new manner that Waugh had explored in an unfinished novel, *Work Suspended* (1942); and it exploited, for the first time, the novelist's religion as a main element in its theme. *Brideshead* was immediately preceded by *Put Out More Flags* (1942). This broadly satirical work described the first year of the war as it influenced the lives of a number of thirties types; it was filled, to use Waugh's phrase, with the spirit of the "Churchillian renaissance." Three works that followed *Brideshead,* the Guy Crouchback novels —*Men at Arms* (1952), *Officers and Gentlemen* (1955), and *Unconditional Surrender* (1961)*—were based on Waugh's actual wartime experience. This trilogy represents, I believe, the most notable achievement of his later career. In 1965 Waugh issued a "recension" of the three works, in one volume, under the title *Sword of Honour.*

A series of short works and a saint's life also followed the war. Waugh wrote *Scott-King's Modern Europe* (1947) after

* The American title, regrettably, is *The End of the Battle.*

a journey to Spain,[6] but this satire of a totalitarian Balkan state more nearly suggests Yugoslavia. *The Loved One* (1948) resulted from a visit to the United States, where Waugh, like Aldous Huxley, was repelled by the wonders of Forest Lawn Cemetery and by the mores of Hollywood. *Love Among the Ruins* (1953), another short piece, follows both Huxley and George Orwell into the totalitarian future, protesting the shape of things as they are by prophesying the shape of things to come. *Helena* (1950) was the second of Waugh's saint's lives; his first, *Edmund Campion* (1935), a biography of the Elizabethan Catholic martyr, had won the Hawthornden Prize. The novel *Helena* is a very modern saint's life, complete with contemporary English slang; it narrates the "invention" of the cross by the mother of the Emperor Constantine, a lady Waugh imagines to have been a Briton.

In the late fifties Waugh published a short novel, *The Ordeal of Gilbert Pinfold* (1957), and a biography, *The Life of Ronald Knox* (1959). The latter of these is the biography of Waugh's friend, Monsignor Ronald Knox, a fellow convert and a minor satirist. Like *Edmund Campion,* it is notable for the pellucidy of its prose, but it seems to me to be somewhat limited by its subject and pious occasion; it lacks dramatic and psychological intensity. The earlier and more interesting work, *Pinfold,* is in part an autobiographical account of a "brief attack of hallucinations" that, according to his publisher's statement on the jacket of the novel, Waugh underwent in 1954. Subtitled *A Conversation Piece, Pinfold* gives us an engaging self-portrait of the artist in late middle age. Moreover, it rises to moments of grotesque terror during Pinfold's hallucinatory crisis.

Among the satirist's most recent works are *Tourist in Africa* (1960), "Basil Seal Rides Again" (1963), and *A Little Learning* (1964). The first of these, a journal of a Mediterranean and African tour, is far mellower in its social and political observations than the travel books Waugh wrote in the thirties. The short story "Basil Seal Rides Again" also resumes an interest of the 1930's; the handsome limited edition does not compensate for its portrait of that great rogue Basil Seal as an aging, respectable, and anxious father. Both of these are very slight things, indeed. But *A Little Learning,* the first volume of an autobiography, is one of Evelyn Waugh's finest books, possibly because, at last, he has a "life subject" commensurate in interest with the distinction of his prose. That prose, in *A Little Learning,* is all at the top of Waugh's form; entirely easy and natural, it is urbane, witty, allusive, precise, graceful—responsive to every modulation of narrative and dialogue he wishes to express. The account of Waugh's childhood, youth, and young manhood is a fascinating social record of the early decades of the century and of a culture now gone forever. Even should the subsequent volumes of this autobiography disappoint us, the section on Waugh's preparatory and public school days should join George Orwell's "Such, Such Were the Joys . . ." as a classic account of the experience of an upper-class English boy at school in the early years of this century.

Though hostile to "psychological" explanations of character, as he is to many "modern" tendencies, Evelyn Waugh has also given us, in this autobiographical volume, meaningful insights into the conditions from which his art has developed. His warm description of the contented years in the nursery, his intense recollection of the shock occasioned by his departure from home to school, his evident delight as he evokes memories of the favorite house of his childhood, his aunts' mid-Victorian one at Midsomer Norton, confirm one's impressions of the importance of certain motifs of childhood innocence and symbolic architecture in his satires. In fact, in mournfully reflecting on the obliteration of the rural world of his childhood and in describing the "grim cyclorama of spoliation which surrounded all English experience in this century," Evelyn Waugh strikes off a phrase that might serve as epigraph to his entire career: "To have been born into a world of beauty, to die amid ugliness, is the common fate of all us exiles."

But biographical criticism has its pitfalls, as J. B. Priestley inadvertently revealed a number of years ago in his review of *The Ordeal of Gilbert Pinfold.* Obviously identifying Pinfold with Waugh, whose marriage to a member of the aristocracy and residency at Piers Court, Stinchcombe, a Gloucestershire manor house, were common knowledge, Priestley scolded, "He is trying to be the country gentleman, when he is, in fact, the artist; he is trying to detach himself from the life of the nation, when he should involve himself in it." Priestley then added a terrible and tasteless warning: if the artist continues to deny his real self, he will have another bout of hallucinations. "Pinfold must step out of his role as a Cotswold gentleman quietly regretting the Reform Bill of 1832."[7] Thus confusing life and art, Priestley failed to see that Evelyn Waugh, in common with all satirists and in the manner of his persona Gilbert Pinfold, who masked himself as "a combination of eccentric don and testy colonel," has always played a role for the sake of his art—not at its expense. Ironically enough, a few years after Priestley's warning, Evelyn Waugh went on to publish the last volume of his Crouchback trilogy in which his hero refuses to identify himself with the life of the nation but does identify himself with life—a fortunate marriage and many children!

Indeed, considering that Waugh's complete autobiography is not yet available and reflecting upon all the graces of its first volume, I think that an attempt to interpret Waugh's satires now in terms of his biography, or his biography in terms of his satires, would be wildly presumptuous. Even Frederic Stopp's interesting *Evelyn Waugh: Portrait of an Artist* (1958) is at its best, not in the scanty biographical chapters or in the passages of Jungian analysis, but in its comments on details of the novels. In the pages that follow, therefore,

I have not sought to illuminate Evelyn Waugh's psyche or his life. I do hope that I have related Waugh to significant literary, spiritual, and political tendencies of his period and that, to some degree, I have illuminated his central motifs, his satiric techniques and attitudes, and his development as an artist.

A NOTE ON SATIRE

Modern satire is not a genre but an attitude toward man and society that may be given expression, by means of certain traditional techniques, in any literary form. As Northrop Frye has observed, the idea of satire as a distinct form in English literature is a renaissance and neoclassical idea; "it hardly existed in the middle ages, and it hardly exists now."[8] In the novel, as in other forms, satire may be given different degrees of emphasis: the spirit of satire may lightly brush the surface of a novel; it may lend a pronounced color to other significant elements; it may deeply suffuse the whole.

Elaborate systems of classification are occasionally advanced to explain these different degrees of satiric emphasis, but the one essential distinction we need to make is between the novel with some satiric elements and the satiric novel. There are, for instance, satiric touches throughout E. M. Forster's *Passage to India.* James Joyce employs satiric techniques—indeed, dazzles us with them—in *Ulysses.* But these novels are not regarded, customarily, as satires, because the satirical elements are in no sense dominant. For that matter, even the satirical novelist is not necessarily satirical all the time, nor always to the same degree. Aldous Huxley's *The Genius and the Goddess* was not satirical at all by comparison to one of his more successful early works, such as *Antic Hay*; and satire in Waugh's *Brideshead Revisited* was subordinated to other elements to a degree that readers of his earlier works might not have imagined possible. But when a novelist constantly deploys characters, contrives incidents, arranges episodes, and employs rhetorical devices so that his total effect and articulated theme are satirical, he belongs to the class of satirical novelists.

The word "novel" is, of course, a catch-all term, but it is inescapable: we use it even knowing that we should make more precise distinctions. Properly speaking, Evelyn Waugh's early novels are satiric romances, with some of the qualities of the novel. His later works, particularly the Crouchback trilogy, in which he approaches probability and verisimilitude, are a satirical blend of novel and romance. There were some traces of another fictional form, the Menippean satire—the form of Rabelais, of Swift in *Gulliver's Travels,* of Voltaire in *Candide,* of Norman Douglas in *South Wind,* of Huxley in *Crome Yellow*—in the early Waugh, but these traces reveal themselves more in his attitude toward man in society than in the structure of his books. In his early works the ironic attitude associated with Menippean satire was assimilated by the romance form. (In the early Huxley, by contrast, Menippean satire tended to assimilate the romance.*) In this respect, the influence of Ronald Firbank, who wrote satiric romance rather than Menippean satire, was of paramount importance in Waugh's development.

Satire, both as a term and as a means of expression, constantly provokes controversy. Many discussions are unsatisfactory because they are based on a priori views of what satire can do and must be. But it is impossible to prescribe the exact nature of a spirit that has endured in various prose forms since the time of the Greeks. Sometimes satire aims to correct or reform; but probably even more often satire is written, as Wyndham Lewis argued it could be, for its own

* See the discussion of the forms of prose fiction in Northrop Frye's *Anatomy of Criticism* (Princeton, N. J., 1957), for a full and lucid treatment of the differences among novel, romance, and Menippean satire.

sake. Sometimes humor is a recognizable element of satire. But the range of satire, and its techniques of expression, are so extensive that within the satiric speculum are various shadings of the comic, the grotesque, the shocking, and the disgusting. Sometimes satire is a purely destructive force; but just as often it is creative too.

One need only consult the recent symposium, "Norms, Moral or Other, in Satire,"[9] to see how widely experts may disagree on the question of the satirist's positive values and the role they play in satire. The conflicting evidence presented by the writers involved in this symposium suggests that it would be wise to avoid arbitrary assumptions and dogmatic attitudes. Instances can be piled up ad infinitum to demonstrate that sometimes satire has been explicitly moralistic; that sometimes it gives absolutely no hint of positive standards; that sometimes it simultaneously punishes folly and vice and reveals virtue.

Whatever else the satirist may be, he is a man who cannot help but expose foolishness and vice and absurdity; and he does have standards (whether they be personal, social, political, theological, moral, aesthetic, or metaphysical) by which he judges, even if those standards remain implicit rather than explicit in his writing. He must know some "good" if he is to expose and ridicule man's imperfections. He is at his best when his own sense of the "good" is neither crude nor confused. When his medium is the novel, the satirist is not compelled by any law to pursue a particular course: satirically forceful and aesthetically satisfying novels have been produced by writers who have tended almost completely to conceal their "norms" or positive values, and also by writers who, while eschewing propaganda, apology, and didacticism, embodied their "norms" in detail, symbol, character, and incident.

Contents

PART FIVE: THE PRESENT AGE AND THE PASSING ORDER

Part One

IN THE WASTE LAND

CHAPTER I

Waugh and the Tradition of the Satirical Novel

PURITANS have found him frivolous; or, at best, they have seen him as an "entertainer." But Evelyn Waugh has never been trivial, and he has always been much more than merely entertaining. Indeed, he is one of the truly accomplished figures of the modern period, a writer who provides a startling insight into the nature of the times. His art may lack the depth and range we associate with the greatest moderns, but his wit, acuteness, and craftsmanship compel respect. In *The Ordeal of Gilbert Pinfold,* an admittedly autobiographical work, Waugh describes his novelist hero in this genial manner:

> It may happen in the next hundred years that the English novelists of the present day will come to be valued as we now value the artists and craftsmen of the late eighteenth century. The originators, the exuberant men, are extinct and in their place subsists and modestly flourishes a generation notable for elegance and variety and contrivance....
>
> Among these novelists Mr. Gilbert Pinfold stood quite high. At . . . the age of fifty, he had written a dozen books all of which were still bought and read. . . . Foreign students often chose them as the subject for theses, but those who sought to detect cosmic significance in Mr. Pinfold's work, to relate it to fashions in philosophy, social predicaments or psychological tensions were baffled by his frank, curt replies to their questionnaires; their fellows in the English Literature Schools, who chose more egotistical writers, often found their theses more than half

composed for them. Mr. Pinfold gave nothing away. Not that he was secretive or grudging by nature; he had nothing to give these students. He regarded his books as objects which he had made, things external to himself to be used and judged by others. He thought them well made, better than many reputed works of genius, but he was not vain of his accomplishments, still less of his reputation.

This evaluation of Gilbert Pinfold's position in relation to the literary stream of the present half century is a modest and just assessment of Waugh's own standing. Some readers would insist, however, that not only are Evelyn Waugh's books better made than those of more highly reputed writers but that a number of his works possess an underlying seriousness of theme which also marks them as superior. As G. S. Fraser has observed, Waugh's novels of the thirties are among those works "written superficially in terms of comedy or even farce, but with an underlying very disturbing note of bitterness which emphasized the ruthlessness, the nerviness, the unhappiness, the lack of purpose and the lack of love, in much contemporary British life."[1] In fact, Waugh has always been a writer whose surface—apparently gay, sometimes bizarre, often even wildly uproarious—has masked a devastating satirical vision of the modern world.

It seems doubtful that Evelyn Waugh would have written with such assurance as he manifests in even the first of his satirical novels had he not been in touch with a tradition of sophisticated romance pervaded by the spirit of satire.* Though Waugh, unlike Aldous Huxley, did not model his novels on the Menippean satire of Norman Douglas, he did find in *South Wind* (1917)—a work that his hero Charles Ryder prominently displayed in his room at Oxford—elements to attract him: the detached, disdainful attitude of superior-

* In *Satire and Fiction* (London, n.d.), Wyndham Lewis sensibly observed that "No work of fiction . . . is likely to be only 'satire' in the sense that a short epigrammatic piece, in rhyming couplets (an epistle of Pope), would be." Yet most of the novels of Evelyn Waugh, Aldous Huxley, and Wyndham Lewis are so pervaded by the spirit of satire and its techniques that I do not hesitate to apply either the term "satirical novel" or "satire" to them.

ity, of course, but more particularly the calculated outrageousness. Consider just this one sentence from *South Wind*: "The funeral was a roaring success." Surely Waugh echoes these words and even the tone when he writes, "Whatever the reason, the wedding was certainly an unparalleled success among the lower orders."

But Ronald Firbank was a more important influence on the satires of Evelyn Waugh. Writing in 1929, Waugh noted that, although Firbank's earlier books might tend to be "silly" and "obscure," certain of the later novels reveal "radiant lucidity" and a silliness that is "exquisitely significant."* In truth, although Firbank drew his raw material from the nineties of Oscar Wilde and Aubrey Beardsley, a sharp ironic impulse qualified his decadence and sentimentalism. From this fruitful tension sprang the pronounced satirical quality of his best works. His satires are antithetical to a work such as *South Wind,* for Firbank works by indirection. He has no interest in ideas; he is no reformer. Nevertheless, through the indirection of his irony and by means of a montage-like technique, Firbank achieves some intense effects.

In an excellent essay, Evelyn Waugh states that those who dislike Firbank must also be hostile "to a wide and vigorous tendency in modern fiction."[2] And, in fact, Firbank did make important technical contributions to the novel—in the handling of dialogue, in experiments with structure, and in certain elements of comic organization.

First of all, Firbank reduced narration and description to a minimum, relying primarily upon dialogue. In his use of dialogue, he was remarkably inventive. His particular mannerisms of stichomythia, innuendo, incompleted sentences,

* Evelyn Waugh, "Ronald Firbank," *Life and Letters*, II (March, 1929), 192. Though Waugh, much later in his career, had words of high praise for P. G. Wodehouse, this essay and the evidence of the novels point to Firbank as his true master. In a *Paris Review* interview (Summer-Fall, 1963), Waugh states that parts of *Vile Bodies*, a book he disparages, were "cribbed" from Firbank and that he admired that writer "very much when I was young." He adds, however, "I think there would be something wrong with an elderly man who could enjoy Firbank."

and ellipses revealed to others the flexibility and suggestiveness long passages of uninterrupted dialogue might have. Waugh's indebtedness to certain Firbankian techniques can be easily demonstrated. Let us examine some passages from Firbank's *Valmouth* (1919) and *The Flower Beneath the Foot* (1923). In the first passage, below, Mrs. Hurstpierpoint, a centenarian, and Mrs. Thoroughfare, a dowager, have just noticed a village swain. Father Colley-Mahoney speaks:

"How . . . if the glorious Virgin required you to take this young fellow under your wing?"

Mrs. Hurstpierpoint bent thoughtfully her eyes to the somewhat "phallic" pessementerie upon her shawl.

"For the sake, I presume," she queried, "of his soul?"

"Precisely."

"But is he ripe?" Mrs. Thoroughfare wondered.

"Ripe?"

"I mean——"

There was a busy silence.

This is Laura de Nazianzi and her friend, Olga:

"I would give all my soul to him, Rara . . . my chances of heaven!"

"Your chances, Olga——" Mademoiselle de Nazianzi murmured, avoiding some bird-droppings with her skirt.

"How I envy *the men*, Rara, in his platoon!"

"Take away his uniform, Olga, and what does he become?"

"Ah, *what*——!"

These same devices of italicized words, ellipses, suggestive fragments, and sly implications appear in the satires of Evelyn Waugh. His Kitty Blackwater and Fanny Throbbing, two Edwardian dames in *Vile Bodies,* would be perfectly at ease among the ladies of Firbank's *Valmouth.* Consider the following passage:

"Fanny, surely that is Agatha Runcible, poor Viola Chasm's daughter"

"I wonder Viola allows her to go about like that. If she were my daughter . . ."

"*Your* daughter, Fanny . . ."

"Kitty, that was not kind."

(Fanny's daughter, we have already learned, quite by indirection, had been procured by Margot Beste-Chetwynde for prostitution in South America.) Kitty responds:

"Darling, I'm sorry. . . . I can't help thinking . . . girls seem to know so much nowadays. We had to learn everything for ourselves, didn't we, Fanny, and it took so long. If I'd had Agatha Runcible's chances. . . . Who is that young man with her?"

"I don't know, and, frankly, I don't think, do you? . . . He has that self contained look."

"He has very nice eyes. And he moves well."

"I dare say when it came to the point. . . . Still as I said, if I had had Agatha Runcible's advantages. . . ."

Later, these ladies are at it again:

"Who is that very important young man?" asked Mrs. Blackwater of Lady Throbbing.

"I don't know, dear. He bowed to *you.*"

"He bowed to you, dear."

"How very nice. . . . I wasn't quite sure. . . . He reminds me a little of dear Prince Anrep."

"It's so nice in these days to see someone who really looks . . . don't you think?"

"You mean the beard?"

"The beard among other things, darling."

Those long passages of overheard fragments and snatches of conversation that Firbank liked to compose in an impressionist manner also were useful to Waugh. This passage from *Valmouth,* a jumble of voices at a party, is typical:

"Heroin."

"Adorable simplicity."

"What could anyone find to admire in such a shelving profile?"

"We reckon a duck here of two or three and twenty not so old. And a spring chicken *anything to fourteen.*"

"My husband had no amorous energy whatsoever: which just suited me, of course."

As late as *Brideshead Revisited* Waugh still found this mocking device useful, though characteristically he imposed tighter control over it. The conversation of Rex Mottram and his friends just before the war may also be influenced by the dialogue in T. S. Eliot's *Sweeney Agonistes,* but its primary indebtedness is to Firbank:

> "The press are with him."
> "I'm with him."
> "Who cares about divorce now except for a few old maids who aren't married, anyway?"
> "If he has a showdown with the old gang, they'll just disappear like, like. . . ."
> "Why don't we close the Canal? Why didn't we bomb Rome?"
> "It wouldn't have been necessary. One firm note. . . ."
> "One firm speech."
> "One showdown."
> "Anyway, Franco will soon be skipping back to Morocco. Chap I saw to-day just back from Barcelona. . . ."
> ". . . Chap just back from Fort Belvedere. . . ."

Ronald Firbank also made, as I have suggested, a most important contribution to the structure of the novel. Evelyn Waugh says that Firbank was the first of the modern novelists to solve the problem of representation in fiction because he remained "objective" and yet built up his "compositions" so that occasionally "a brief visual image flashes out to illumine and explain the flickering succession of spoken words." In reducing narration and description to a minimum and in developing his novels through a series of vignettes rather than a coherent action, Firbank found, according to Waugh, "a new balanced interrelation of subject and form." In effect, Firbank, who was possibly not entirely conscious of what he was doing, devised the technique of "counterpoint" which was to become a major device of Aldous Huxley and Evelyn Waugh. The novelists of the nineteenth century, Waugh argued in his Firbank essay, were bound by the arbitrary convention of the succession of events in a cause-to-effect relationship. Firbank's use of counterpoint, then, was of central importance, providing a technical precedent for Huxley, who found in counterpoint a way to express his irony and to escape from the chronology he despised, and for Waugh, who perceived that a sequence of events in a cause-to-effect relationship could not express, except as a special device in the midst of "counterpoint," the absurdity he saw in English society of the thirties.[3]

Finally, Firbank developed a comic technique of setting off a silly and inconsequential chain of events and then burying further reference to the chain in the midst of other material. Evelyn Waugh employed this booby-trap device to achieve some of his most characteristic effects. He draws our attention, with evident delight, to Firbank's handling of the device in *The Flower Beneath the Foot.*[4] At dinner Lady Something imperfectly overhears the sentence, "I could not be more astonished . . . if you told me there were fleas at the Ritz." After several chapters, suddenly in the midst of a conversation, we find:

> "Had I known, Lady Something, I was going to be ill, I would have gone to the Ritz!" the Hon. "Eddy" gasped.
>
> "And you'd have been bitten all over!" Lady Something replied.

Then, pages after this bit of foolishness, we come across this:

> "Guess who is at the Ritz, ma'am, this week!" the Countess demurely murmured.
>
> "Who is at this Ritz this week, I can't," the Queen replied.
>
> "Nobody."

And so it goes.

As Waugh develops this technique in his early satire, it is even more pointed, and it reveals a world grotesque and cruel, without purpose or meaning. In *Decline and Fall,* for instance, little Lord Tangent is accidentally wounded during the bogus school games. Eventually a passing reference is made to the swelling of his foot. Then we learn, pages later, that, "Everybody" was at Grimes's wedding, "except little Lord Tangent, whose foot was being amputated at a local nursing home." Finally, in a description of public reaction to the anticipated wedding of Margot and Paul, Lady Circumference says: "It's maddenin' Tangent having died just at this time. . . . People may think that that's my reason for refusin'." In the same novel the incidents that lead to Mr. Prendergast's slaying by a lunatic with a saw are presented in this manner, as is the chain of events leading to the death of Miss Runcible in *Vile Bodies* and of Prudence in *Black Mischief,* and to the ruin and exile of Ambrose Silk in *Put Out More Flags.* Certainly Evelyn Waugh learned his lesson well at the school of Ronald Firbank, for in Waugh this comic trick reveals significant silliness and something more—his essential attitude toward the nature of his time.

Firbank's objectivity and detachment, the counterpoint or montage technique which was his essential mode of presentation, the subtlety of his dialogue, which proceeds through understatement, suggestive emphasis, and sly innuendo, the inventiveness of his comic devices, provided the young Waugh with a model for an economical, destructive, and nondidactic satire. The influence was a fortunate one, for, in alliance with Waugh's innate satirical genius, it contributed to the development of techniques more purely artful than those found in either Aldous Huxley or Wyndham Lewis. If Waugh's satires lack the intellectual brilliance of Huxley's or the fury of Lewis', they reveal a degree of control and craftsmanship such as Huxley and Lewis seldom attained. That control and artistry, though severely strained by developments in his later career which I shall note, gave to Waugh a staying power that his contemporary satirical novelists lacked.

CHAPTER II

Change and Decay

THE most extraordinary quality of Waugh's first satire, *Decline and Fall,* is that in the world he depicts nothing has any meaning at all, for cause has only the most irrational relation to effect and the greatest disparity exists between action and consequence. Paul Pennyfeather, sent down from Oxford for "indecent behavior"—he was debagged by a group of drunken aristocrats—takes the inevitable step for one in his situation and becomes a schoolteacher at Llanabba in Wales. Next Paul is carried off by Margot Beste-Chetwynde, who makes him her lover, and involved by her in the white-slave traffic from which she derives her considerable wealth. Imprisoned for his "crime," Paul is rescued by Margot, who has married Sir Humphrey Maltravers, a cabinet minister; a fake death from appendicitis is staged, and Paul returns to Oxford to resume his preparations for the ministry. He dies, he reappears, but he is not reborn. Nothing that has happened has had any effect upon him.

Moreover, the world into which Paul is tossed after Oxford is a complete sham: "bogus," Waugh's Bright Young People would call it. When the innocent Paul is sentenced to prison for white slavery, the judge remarks that "no one could be ignorant of the callous insolence with which, on the very eve of arrest for this most infamous of crimes, the accused had been preparing to join his name with one honoured in his country's history, and to drag down to his own pitiable depths of depravity a lady of beauty, rank, and stainless reputation." He concludes by characterizing Paul as a "human vampire." It would not be quite correct to identify hypocrisy as the object of the satire, however; for, as Waugh has remarked with considerable asperity, in this century "vice no longer pays lip service to virtue."[1] The judge's rhetoric is primarily absurd because it has so little relevance to the brazen amorality depicted throughout the novel. In the world of *Decline and Fall,* writes Stephen Spender, "there is in reality no Fall, nor sin, nor retribution," no crime "counts" and "no one suffers for his offenses."[2]

The action of the novel, an improbable series of chance encounters, expresses a vision of incoherence. While he is in prison, Paul meets not only his two former colleagues at Llanabba—Grimes (who is in prison for bigamy) and Prendergast (who is now the prison chaplain)—but also Philbrick (the former butler at the school, who is now a prisoner too). Not one of them is the least surprised; all accept the fact, without observation, that life expresses itself in terms of such absurdity. In fact, in the early satires when events follow in some cause-to-effect relation to one another, the events are so shocking and the characters respond to them with such indifference that they are seen to be a part of the incoherence, too. In *Decline and Fall* Waugh permits only one emotional response, by a character, to the gruesome fate of little Lord Tangent, whose foot was grazed by a bullet during some school sports: the relish with which Beste-Chetwynde informs Pennyfeather that Tangent's foot has swollen and turned black.

In similar vein is Agatha Runcible's catastrophe in *Vile Bodies,* Waugh's second satire. Miss Runcible, who has pursued pleasure in an aimless and incoherent way, gets drunk during some auto races the Bright Young People attend. She stumbles into a machine, joins the race, crashes through the fence, and disappears. Later we learn that her car has been wrecked against a village monument. We have a glimpse of Agatha dazed in London, and also see her visited by friends at a nursing home. Subsequently we learn that she has fallen into a coma, and finally a reference is made to her funeral. Neither the author nor the characters make any comment about these events.

Eric Linklater has said that the world Waugh depicts is even tougher than that of Hemingway. Pointing to the "calm acceptance of an irrational, glittering, unjust, and determined sequence of events," Linklater argues that there was logic in Hemingway's toughness but that "behind the infliction of pain and injustice in Mr. Waugh's novels there was nothing but an arbitrary and inscrutable power."[3] Actually, these novels are even more unsettling than Linklater's reading of them, because they do not, in fact, suggest the operation of an inscrutable and deterministic power. On the contrary, they seem to imply that in the valueless and incoherent world where the characters lead their untidy lives no order or purpose is even discernible.

The titles of Waugh's early satires—*Decline and Fall, Vile Bodies, A Handful of Dust*—are important keys to the seriousness of the attitude which informs them. The decay of a civilization, futile sensuality leading to boredom, the poverty of spiritual life—these are the subjects of the first three works, all pointing clearly to the conclusion that during the thirties Waugh, like Aldous Huxley, was much under the influence of the "waste land" view of things. While it cannot be demonstrated that T. S. Eliot influenced Waugh's satirical techniques, Waugh does seem to have shared the disillusionment and disgust to which *The Waste Land* gave quintessential expression. In the political life of the nation, in the institution of the family, in the relation between the sexes, in the spiritual condition of his characters, Waugh discerns only futility and sterility. All coherence is gone from the world he describes, as it is gone from the desolate world of Eliot's poem.

In *Vile Bodies* occasional glimpses of the political life of the country counterpoint the extravagant exploits of the Bright Young People. Instability and inconsequence reign in political affairs just as they do in the lives of the young. Lord Outrage, "last week's Prime Minister," busily plots with Lord Metroland and Father Rothschild, an ubiquitous Jesuit who alone seems to know what is happening in the country. But the new government is defeated, largely in consequence of the Young People's visit to 10 Downing Street, a visit followed by newspaper stories of a midnight orgy and by photographs of Miss Runcible "tumbling down the steps" in a Hawaiian costume. Outrage himself is a Prufrock figure who carries on a futile affair with the wife of the Japanese ambassador. I "really would have brought matters to a crisis," Outrage tells himself, as the Baroness leaves his hotel room in disgust, "if it had not been for that telephone." Not surprisingly, then, in view of this instability and impotence, the novel ends on a battlefield of "unrelieved desolation" where a war involving liquid-fire and leprosy germs is being waged against an unidentified enemy.

The disintegration of order in political life corresponds to the collapse of the family. In *Decline and Fall* Lady Circumference, reflecting on the death of Lord Tangent, is piqued that the public will ascribe her absence at Margot Beste-Chetwynde's wedding to Tangent's death and remain unaware of her desire to snub Margot. In the same novel young Peter Beste-Chetwynde presides over the selection of his mother's lovers. And in *Vile Bodies* the following exchange takes place between Fanny Throbbing and Kitty Blackwater:

> "Why, look, there's Miles."
> "Miles?"
> "Your son, darling. My nephew, you know."

"Miles. Do you know, Kitty, I believe it is. He never comes to see me now, the naughty boy."

A Handful of Dust depicts the collapse of the family even more incisively. John, the son of Tony and Brenda, is deposited with a nurse and a groom for companionship and training; and when Brenda learns that her son, John Andrew, rather than her lover, John Beaver, has died in an accident, she exclaims, "John . . . John Andrew . . . I . . . Oh, thank God. . . ." Less direct than these frontal assaults on the irresponsibility of parents is the implicit comment the novels make on the disintegration of the English family: divorce or separation figure prominently in at least five of Waugh's satires; adultery in at least seven. (A later novel that concerns a family as a unit—*Brideshead Revisited*—traces that family's violent dissolution.)

While the administration of the nation's political life resides with the emotionally impotent Lord Outrage and the base Lord Metroland (who waits in the library to avoid meeting his wife's lover on the staircase), and while the family as an effective moral unit crumbles, the Bright Young People surrender to an endless round of parties and sterile amours. Although Evelyn Waugh's sympathy is with them to a significant degree, he is fully aware of their weaknesses. In an article published in 1929 he speaks of his generation as "undiscriminating" and "ineffectual," and argues that nine hundred fifty in every thousand "are totally lacking in any sense of qualitative value." Given the contemporary absence of direction, order, and restraint, youth had only "one thing left to rebel against—the idea of mere decency."[4] In fact, in the earlier novels the only influential values in English society are purely synthetic ones, such as those created by the gossip columns of the newspapers or by the attitudes of the smart set. For example, in *Vile Bodies* Adam is able to create a demand for black suede evening shoes and for invitations from an imaginary hostess; and in *A Handful of Dust,* when Polly Cockpurse's set gives its stamp of approval to Brenda's affair with Beaver, "Beaver, for the first time in his life, found himself a person of interest and, almost of consequence."

The ultimate effect of this inadequate sense of values is an inadequate relationship between man and woman—another echo of T. S. Eliot's *The Waste Land.* Waugh's most devastating exploration of this theme is not the affair of Adam and Nina, which is at least based on real love, but the adultery of Brenda Last and John Beaver. Brenda embarks on her "affair" with a young man she knows perfectly well to be "second rate and a snob and . . . cold as a fish," purely out of boredom; Beaver, for his part, is interested in the social and financial advantages which he hopes will accrue to him.

While Evelyn Waugh is usually spoken of now as a Catholic novelist, his early novels—all, excepting *Decline and Fall,* written after his conversion—reveal no explicit Catholicism; and not until *Brideshead Revisited* did his religion figure as a theme in his fiction. Nevertheless, the fact of his conversion and the choice of a phrase from Eliot's poem as the title of his third novel indicate that he was aware, early in his career, of the condition of religion in the modern world. *Decline and Fall* treats the subject of religion lightly; both Paul Pennyfeather and Mr. Prendergast are ludicrous. Paul, after the incredible and unedifying experience to which he is subjected, returns to Oxford and resumes, under another identity, his theological training, altogether unaffected by what has happened to him. He is destined to be a conventional and perfectly useless clergyman.

Waugh paints the satirical portrait of Mr. Prendergast in even broader strokes. Prendy, a completely ineffectual master and the butt of the boys' jokes, confides to Paul that his state has not always been so low; he should have been a "a rector with [his] . . . own house and bathroom." In fact, he continues, he "might have been a rural dean, only [he] . . . had

Doubts." Installed in a chintz bedecked rectory, suddenly, in the midst of a conversation with guests, Prendergast was overwhelmed by his Doubts: not the ordinary "sort of Doubt about Cain's wife or the old Testament miracles or the consecration of Bishop Parker," that he had been taught to explain away in college, but "something deeper than all that." Poor Prendergast *"couldn't understand why God had made the world at all."* And so, in spite of his bishop's reassurance that his Doubts need not affect his duties as a parish priest, Prendergast resigned his living. Later, in prison, Paul re-encounters him; now the prison chaplain, Prendy has discovered that it is possible to be "a species of person called a 'Modern Churchman' " and to draw the full salary of a beneficed clergyman while remaining uncommitted to any religious belief. In this role Prendergast is no more effective than as a schoolmaster, for he has discovered that "criminals are just as bad as boys." There is a touch of cruelty in this portrait of Prendergast, who is made to seem absurd for some decent qualities, such as his impulse to resign; but the basis for the satirical portrait of both Paul and the modern churchman is that neither has anything real in which to believe.

In *Vile Bodies* the satirical treatment of bogus religion and of irreligion is both more complex and more central to the novel. Father Rothschild is a grotesque figure who travels with a false beard and manipulates the political career of Lord Outrage. And even though the Father is the only character in the novel who seems to have some understanding of the chaos around him, he is himself implicated in that disorder.

While Father Rothschild plots happily behind the scenes, Mrs. Melrose-Ape, an American evangelist, moves very much to the forefront, surrounded by her "angels"—Faith, Charity, Chastity, Humility, Prudence, Divine Discontent, Mercy, Justice, and Creative Endeavour—who have accompanied her on a revivalist tour of England and who, it must be admitted, are less interested in God than in Man. Mrs. Melrose-Ape (whose name has something to do with our attitude toward her) is a purveyor of a debased faith and is something less than angelic herself. She has "favorites" among the angels, and a suggestion of abnormality attaches to her. When she first appears, during a rough crossing of the channel, "nothing if not 'magnetic,' " she assures the angels that, "If you have peace in your hearts your stomach will look after itself," and then "squaring her shoulders and looking (except that she had really no beard to speak of) every inch a sailor, strode resolutely forrard to the first-class bar."

Yet when Mrs. Ape appears in Margot Metroland's ballroom before the smart set and the Bright Young People, we discover that even the debased coin she carries can, for a moment, make the guests uncomfortable:

> Then Mrs. Melrose-Ape stood up to speak. A hush fell in the ballroom beginning at the back and spreading among the gilt chairs until only Mrs. Blackwater's voice was heard exquisitely articulating some details of Lady Metroland's past. Then she, too, was silent and Mrs. Ape began her oration about Hope.
>
> "Brothers and Sisters," she said in a hoarse, stirring voice. Then she paused and allowed her eyes, renowned throughout three continents for their magnetism, to travel among the gilded chairs. (It was one of her favorite openings.) "*Just you look at yourselves,*" she said.
>
> Magically, self-doubt began to spread in the audience.

But just as Mrs. Panrast fears that her unseemly advances to Chastity will be exposed; and Miss Runcible, incorrigible to the end, wonders if her nose is powdered; and Nina mourns her lost innocence; and Lady Throbbing thinks of her past; just as Creative Endeavour concludes that "She's got 'em again"; suddenly "on that silence vibrant with self accusation broke the organ voice of England, the hunting cry of the *ancien régime*":

> Lady Circumference gave a resounding snort of disapproval:
>
> "What a damned impudent woman," she said.
>
> Adam and Nina and Miss Runcible began to giggle, and Margot

Metroland for the first time in her many parties was glad to realize that the guest of the evening was going to be a failure. It had been an awkward moment.

The satire in this episode cuts in several different directions. What Mrs. Ape has to offer is transparently inadequate, but the giggles and the relief following on Lady Circumference's shattering words indicate the need for some kind of rebirth, if not for the kind Mrs. Ape has in mind.

No rebirth could possibly come from the religion of Tony Last or, in fact, from the church he attends, as Waugh describes them in *A Handful of Dust.* Tony, the most sympathetic of Waugh's early heroes, has made regular attendance at church on Sunday morning one of the minor rituals that bring gladness to his heart. The "mildly ceremonious order of his Sunday mornings," Waugh writes, had "evolved from the more severe practice of his parents." The tone of the satire, indulgent as it treats such rituals as Tony's Sunday visit to the greenhouse, sharpens in its representation of the Anglican service. The local vicar, who had been given the living at the instance of Tony's father's dentist, is an elderly man, retired from India. He is renowned for the quality of his voice:

His sermons had been composed in his more active days for delivery at the garrison chapel; he had done nothing to adapt them to the changed conditions of his ministry and they mostly concluded with reference to homes and dear ones far away. The villagers did not find this in any way surprising. Few of the things said in church seemed to have any particular reference to themselves.

So it is with Tony, too; indeed, none of the ritual seems to have any particular reference to him. Consequently,

. . . as Tony inhaled the agreeable slightly musty atmosphere and performed the familiar motions of sitting, standing, and leaning forward, his thoughts drifted from subject to subject, among the events of the past week and his plans for the future. Occasionally some arresting phrase in the liturgy would recall him to his surroundings, but for the most part that morning he occupied himself with the question of bathrooms and lavatories, and of how more of them could best be introduced without disturbing the character of the house.

The complete dissociation of "religion" from the rest of life is brought home with terrible irony at the accidental death of Tony's son. The vicar visits the master of Hetton and tries to be comforting, and Tony later says, "It was very painful, . . . after all the last thing one wants to talk about at a time like this is religion." Unfortunately, he does count on falling back upon his wife Brenda, who, unknown to him, is in London carrying on a love affair.

Waugh's later novels have not so directly satirized the inadequate religious life of modern society as did *Decline and Fall, Vile Bodies,* and *A Handful of Dust.* Certainly his attitude toward civilization has not changed; if anything, his sense of our time as a waste land of the spirit has grown more intense and pervasive. But he has tended to focus upon the influence on the lives of his characters of Catholicism in conflict with the contemporary world, or indirectly to expose the pervasive materialism of this half century. *The Loved One,* a short novel inspired by the famous Forest Lawn Cemetery of Los Angeles, follows the latter procedure; it is subtitled *An Anglo-American Tragedy,* and the detachment of its conception and treatment chills.

In an essay entitled "Death in Hollywood," Waugh has made explicit the attitudes reflected in *The Loved One.* He argues that archeologists who visit Los Angeles a thousand years from now will find that "the great cultural decline" of the twentieth century began in the graveyards. Waugh finds the meaning of Forest Lawn Cemetery in its founder's determination to ignore the old customs of death, the "grim traditional alternatives of Heaven and Hell," promising instead immediate and perpetual happiness to the inmates of the cemetery. Herbert Eaton, according to Waugh, was the first man "to offer salvation at an inclusive charge as part of his undertaking service." All the sickening customs of the contemporary mortuary point to an unmistakable conclusion, Waugh asserts, that the old values of hell, purgatory, and physical decay have been reversed. "The body does not decay; it lives on, more chic in death than ever before . . . the soul goes straight from the Slumber Room to Paradise, where it enjoys an endless infancy."[5]

The Loved One gives concrete form to these views as it builds up a picture of an institution devoted to evading reality and to substituting a decadent materialism for traditional moral concepts. The vulgar slogans that greet the visitor (ENTER STRANGER AND BE HAPPY); the moral earnestness with which Mr. Joyboy, Senior Mortician, discusses his craft; the artistic pleasure he and Aimée Thanatogenos take in a nicely drained skull and "supple" flesh—these details both repel and amuse.

The action that Waugh dramatizes in this macabre setting extends the implications of the satire. Aimée Thanatogenos, for whom Mr. Joyboy makes all his corpses smile, is a cosmetician at Whispering Glades, completely devoted to her calling and overjoyed to learn that she has been recommended to become the first female embalmer at the institution. In her eyes, Dennis Barlow, who has come to arrange the burial of a friend, discerns "a rich glint of lunacy." Unattracted by the standard American product, Barlow sees in her what he has sought during his lonely exile from England: "a decadent." Torn between Dennis (who makes "unethical" appeals) and the Mom-dominated Joyboy, Aimée turns for advice to the Guru Brahmin, a certain Mr. Slump who writes a column for the lovelorn. Slump, in a moment of pique, recommends that she "go take a high jump." But Aimée is linked by "an umbilical cord of cafes and fruit shops, of ancestral shady business (fencing and pimping) . . . to the high places of her race." And so, communing with "the spirits of her ancestors, the impious and haunted race who had deserted the altar of the old Gods," and prompted, perhaps even by "Attic voices," to "a higher destiny," she injects herself with strychnine in Mr. Joyboy's workroom.

In Aimée, Waugh depicts a product of our urban ethos; neither the past nor the culture that surrounds her offers her meaningful values. She can turn only to the sham wisdom of the Guru Brahmin, as others turn to the sham paradise of Whispering Glades, and to the unconscious promptings of a racial memory linking her to a dead tradition. Her suicide is inevitable; neither the debased, materialist present nor the dead past can sustain her alien and rootless spirit.

It should be noted, too, that *The Loved One* is an Anglo-American tragedy and that Dennis is also decadent. He came, we read, "from a generation which enjoys a vicarious intimacy with death," and he is fascinated by Whispering Glades and by all the details of Aimée's profession, just as he is fascinated by her decadence. Though he enjoys a triumph when he leaves Hollywood (bribed by Joyboy, for whom he has disposed of Aimée's corpse in the Happy Hunting Ground incinerator), Dennis is committing his own kind of suicide. His cynicism and his incapacity for feeling mark him as another hollow man.

Waugh's satire, from the beginning, has been directed at serious issues; and by means of the apparent extravagance (beyond which some readers are reluctant to move) the satirist has revealed the excesses and deficiencies of the century. For instance, in *Decline and Fall,* the following colloquy between Lord Circumference and Paul Pennyfeather exposes more than the laughable emptiness of upper-class conversation and thought:

> "Fond of sport, eh?" he said. "I mean these sort of sports?"
> "Oh, yes," said Paul. "I think they're so good for the boys."
> "Do you? Do you think that?" said Lord Circumference very earnestly. . . .
> "Yes," said Paul; "don't you?"
> "Me? Yes, oh yes. I think so too. Very good for the boys."

"So useful in case of war or anything," said Paul.

"Do you think so? D'you really think so? That there's going to be another war, I mean?

"Yes. I'm sure of it; aren't you?"

Surely this passage of banal conversation also indicates that in his very first novel, while his gaiety seemed to transfigure all the dreadfulness he depicted, Waugh already had a sense of the inevitable consequence and the significance of the kind of life his characters were leading. It is not surprising, then, that his earliest satires depicted modern times so as to reflect a world without order, coherence, or value, wherein the family was in the process of disintegration; political and spiritual life in a state of decline; the relation between the sexes debased to a peculiarly sterile lust; and the individual passive and rootless, separated from the nourishing traditions of the past. Nor is it surprising that a novelist with such a view of his society, evidently convinced early in his career that his nation was hurtling toward a meaningless war, should have turned—as did the poet of *The Waste Land* himself—to one of the most traditional churches as an alternative to change and decay.

CHAPTER III

England's Stately Houses

FEW readers of the novels of Evelyn Waugh have failed to notice how often the "great house" figures as an important element in the development of theme. Indeed, the values by which Waugh judged his society and his time were first indicated in the Anchorage House passage, one of the contrapuntal contrasts of *Vile Bodies,* arranged so as to imply an evaluation of the Bright Young People and their elders. On the evening that Adam, Nina, Miss Runcible, and the rest attended a party given on the deck of a dirigible, another and quite different party was in progress at Anchorage House:

> This last survivor of the noble town houses of London was, in its time, of dominating and august dimensions, and even now, when it had become a mere "picturesque bit" lurking in a ravine between concrete skyscrapers, its pillared facade, standing back from the street and obscured by railings and some wisps of foliage, had grace and dignity and other-worldliness enough to cause a flutter or two in Mrs. Hoop's heart as she drove into the forecourt.
>
> "Can't you just see the ghosts?" she asked Lady Circumference on the stairs. "Pitt and Fox and Burke and Lady Hamilton and Beau Brummel and Dr. Johnson" (a concurrence of celebrities, it may be remarked, at which something memorable might surely have occurred.)

Lady Circumference, who can manage to see no ghosts, can manage to see many of "the old gang"—Outrage, Metroland, Lady Metroland, Lady Throbbing, Mrs. Blackwater, Mrs.

Mouse. In addition, she finds a group that has not revealed itself in Waugh's pages before:

> . . . a great concourse of pious and honourable people (many of whom made the Anchorage House reception the one outing of the year), their women-folk gowned in rich and durable stuffs, their men ablaze with orders; people who had represented their country in foreign places and sent their sons to die for her in battle, people of decent and temperate life, uncultured, unaffected, unembarrassed, unassuming, unambitious people, of independent judgment and marked eccentricities, kind people who cared for animals and the deserving poor, brave and rather unreasonable people, that fine phalanx of the passing order, approaching, as one day at the Last Trump they hoped to meet their Maker, with decorous and frank cordiality to shake Lady Anchorage by the hand.

This Anchorage House passage is significant, for in it are clustered certain attitudes that help to explain Evelyn Waugh's satirical perspective. First, we must note that Anchorage House appears here as a symbol of graciousness and order, qualities also associated with the pious and honorable concourse. Secondly, the order and restraint of Anchorage House and of its visitors are regarded as remnants of a nobler past; the noble folk belong to a passing order, and Anchorage House is clearly threatened by the encroachment of concrete skyscrapers.

There is about this middle-class writer's dedication to the great house and to the aristocrats who built it something of the same quality of feeling that exists in the poetry of Yeats, another middle-class worshiper of the aristocracy and of the orderly life of its houses. Often Waugh's descriptions of these relics of the past remind the reader of the lines by Yeats, "So let her bridegroom bring her to a house / Where all's accustomed, ceremonious," which invest tradition, custom, ceremony, and order with a beauty at once aesthetic and nobly moral.

The hero of *Work Suspended,* a novelist who is looking for a "house," recognizes that the devotion of people of his generation to domestic architecture is "wistful, half-romantic, half-aesthetic," and he states that "The nobilities of Whig society became, for us, what the Arthurian paladins were in the time of Tennyson." Eric Linklater concludes that Waugh's admiration for noble houses and for the aristocracy is not really a matter of snobbery, but at the same time, he grants that "a certain intolerance may contribute to the degree of this bias." Although it is probably impossible to ignore entirely the element of snobbery in this admiration, Linklater is surely correct in insisting that proper emphasis must fall on the aesthetic attraction.

> In comparison with the chaos of modern life, the integrated and purposeful existence of a nobleman's estate—up till the reign, at any rate, of Edward the Seventh—had an aspect of order and fulfillment which . . . could surely please that sort of aesthetic conscience which requires design not only in statuary but in living.[1]

And finally it must be granted that Waugh invests this orderly way of life with moral significance, too; the visitors to Anchorage House are pious, honorable, plucky, and responsible. So while it is true that class bias has often narrowed the range of Evelyn Waugh's sympathies, it is also true that he has attached definite moral values to the aristocracy he admires.

From the first novel on, however, these aesthetic and moral values are threatened, and terrible things happen to the great house. King's Thursday, which had remained from the reign of Bloody Mary on into this century as the seat of the Earls of Pastmaster, suffers a particularly awful fate in *Decline and Fall.* This country house is a perfect example of Tudor, unmodified by any of the succeeding styles of domestic architecture:

> No wing had been added, no window filled in; no portico, facade, terrace, orangery, tower or battlement marred its timbered front. In the craze for coal gas and indoor sanitation, King's Thursday had slept unscathed by plumber or engineer. The estate carpenter, an office hereditary in the family of the original joiner who had panelled the halls and carved the great staircase, did such restorations as became necessary from time to time for maintenance of the fabric, working with

the same tools and with the traditional methods, so that in a few years his work became almost indistinguishable from that of his grandsires. Rushlights still flickered in the bedrooms.

Visitors to the superb building drive away "in their big motor cars to their modernized manors," and some of them feel that they "have been privileged to step for an hour and a half into the leisurely, prosaic life of the English Renaissance."

But, as expenses mount and servants weaken, it becomes less and less possible to maintain such purity of style. "Modern democracy" calls for "lifts and labour-saving devices," and so Lord Pastmaster, who can bring himself neither to make the changes nor to suffer the discomforts, decides to sell. The purchaser happens to be his sister-in-law, Margot Beste-Chetwynde, who proceeds, as one of the more awful acts in a "many ways disgraceful career," to raze King's Thursday to the ground in favor of a modern house, the creation of Otto Silenus. Given Margot's request for "something clean and square," Otto operates on the assumption that the problem of all contemporary art is "the elimination of the human element from the consideration of form," and produces a factory-like horror. No doubt Waugh satirizes contemporary architecture as one who detests abstract art, admires Pre-Raphaelite painting, and collects Victorian genre paintings; nevertheless, his satirical observation of the dehumanization of certain kinds of "modern" architecture is perceptive. He forces us to recognize, perhaps even against our wishes, that the abstract and the functional can be as lifeless and cold as machinery.

Less damage is done to Hetton Abbey of *A Handful of Dust* than to King's Thursday, but the irony of the Abbey's history wrenches the reader's sensibility more savagely. Hetton, one of the notable houses of the country, had been rebuilt in 1864 in the gothic style. Despised by the country guidebook, by Brenda Last (who is bored with life there), and by visitors who suffer from the discomforts of its Victorian beds, Hetton is a kind of religion to its master, Tony Last, for he devotes his life, his income, and his projected future to the upkeep and improvement of this house. "The lines of its battlements against the sky; the central clock tower where quarterly chimes disturbed all but the heaviest sleepers; the ecclesiastical gloom of the great hall, its ceiling groined and painted in diapers of red and gold . . ." all these he cherishes, as does the author who describes them. The stained glass, the sudden blasts from the ancient furnaces, the glooms and chills of the corridors, the bed chambers, "each named from Mallory, Yseult, Elaine, Mordred and Merlin, Gawaine and Bedivere, Lancelot, Perceval, Tristram, Galahad, his own dressing room, Morgan Le Fay, and Brenda's Guinevere," create for Tony a whole gothic world. Unfortunately, Brenda, after seven years of marriage, is restive and wants a different world. Indeed, it is doubtful whether she can even understand the value that Tony places on his inheritance. She says to him:

> "Well it sometimes seems to me rather pointless keeping up a house this size if we don't now and then ask some other people to stay in it."
>
> *"Pointless?* I can't think what you mean. I don't keep up this house to be a hostel for a lot of bores to come and gossip in. We've always lived here and I hope John will be able to keep it on after me. One has a duty towards one's employees, and towards the place too. It's a definite part of English life which would be a serious loss if. . . ." Then Tony stopped short in his speech and looked at the bed. Brenda had turned on her face and only the top of her head appeared above the sheets.
>
> "Oh God," she said into the pillow. "What have I done?"

Developing one of the most savage ironic contrasts in modern fiction, Waugh plays off Tony's gothic world against the world that centers around the flat Brenda takes when she begins to spend substantial periods of time in London. Mrs. Beaver, the mother of the young man with whom Brenda is becoming involved, is subdividing a small house in Belgravia "into six small flats at three pounds a week, of one room each and a bath." In these flats the "bathrooms are going to be slap-up, with limitless hot water and every transatlantic refinement; the other room would have a large built-in wardrobe . . . and space for a bed." Mrs. Beaver considers that this establishment will "fill a long felt need." And so that Brenda may enjoy the charms of this building, where "after the first flight the staircase changed from marble to faded carpet," Tony sacrifices some of the improvements at Hetton, but not before Brenda has commissioned Mrs. Beaver, whose vulgarity knows no bounds, to mutilate one of Hetton's rooms and to cover its walls with chromium plating.

At the end of the novel, with Tony a prisoner in the Brazilian jungle whence he has fled his wife's perfidy, Hetton still stands, but its earlier glory has grown even dimmer. The death duties have taken their toll, and Tony's cousins are raising Angora rabbits and foxes; the dining hall, the library, and most of the old kitchen quarters are closed, and the family now lives in the morning room, the smoking room, and the former study. In the final irony of this novel, we learn that Teddy Last, who has chosen Galahad as his room, hopes to restore Hetton to "the glory it had enjoyed in the days of his Cousin Tony."

Subsequent novels reveal variations on this theme of the conflict between the order, calm, and tradition of the aristocratic house and the destructive forces of contemporary society. William Boot, the antihero of *Scoop,* is snatched away from the peace and seclusion of Boot Magna Hall, a domicile that sustains (though the Boots are reputedly impoverished) William, his sister and widowed mother, his widowed grandmother, two uncles, seven invalided nurses and domestics, one nurse who can still manage to get around, and ten servants. After being subjected to the excesses of journalism, as a special correspondent for Monomark's *Daily Beast,* and to the disorders of modern political life in Ishmaelia, an African republic, Boot is only too happy to abjure civilization in favor of Nanny Bloggs and the security of Boot Magna.

In *Brideshead Revisited* and the Guy Crouchback novels, the challenge to order and tradition is more insidious than in *Scoop*. Yet, while the position of the great house is more acutely endangered in these works, it is also oddly buttressed by the appearance of a new force. *Brideshead* associates the ideal values of aristocracy—continuity, order, honor—with the Roman Catholic religion. Throughout the novel, Waugh develops with an almost voluptuous care the beauty of the great country seat of the Bridesheads, detailing the loveliness of its gardens, the splendors of its great baroque fountain, the riches of its appointments and furnishings. In the first part of the novel, during the early years of Charles Ryder's friendship with Sebastian Marchmain, the Pre-Raphaelite chapel still burns its sanctuary light. But with the death of Lady Marchmain and the apostasy of Sebastian and Julia, the sacristy lamp is extinguished. Brideshead, without an heir, seems doomed; the modern age has again had its victory—seemingly. However, Sebastian finally finds his way to a monastery, and Julia repents her life of sin, returning to her faith. Ironically or providentially, the Second World War, the modern age in arms, fails to obliterate Brideshead. Though defaced by the troops who have been encamped on the grounds and in the house itself, Brideshead survives, and the sacristy lamp burns once again in the chapel, signifying that the "builders and tragedians" of Brideshead have served a purpose beyond themselves.

Another Catholic house, Broome, the ancestral seat of the devout Crouchbacks, is very much in the background of the Guy Crouchback novels to suggest the contrast between the social and moral decadence of the 1940's and the stability and continuity of the Roman Catholic church. With the Crouchback fortune largely dissipated through no fault of the family, the property reduced to park, house, and home farm, Guy's father has been forced to let Broome to a convent and to take rooms in a seaside hotel for himself. But "the sanctuary lamp still burned at Broome as of old." In effect, in the later novels the fusion of Waugh's religious commitment with his devotion to the house of an aristocratic family reveals itself as a profound pessimism about the fate of the social and cultural values the writer admires, and at the same time as a calm assurance of the survival of his faith in a disorderly age. The rock of Roman Catholic tradition stands firmly, for Waugh, in the midst of social and moral decay.

Part Two

THE DOOM OF YOUTH

CHAPTER IV

The Ingénu *and the Cult of Youth*

THE satirical novelist Nigel Dennis has declared that the literary history of the thirties might be written with "the house of childhood at the center." The "Left-poets" of the time did not really approve of this house: Stephen Spender was telling the young men that "It is too late to stay in those houses your fathers built," and W. H. Auden was demanding "new styles of architecture." For these two, and for Day Lewis as well, the house of childhood was something to escape.[1] Not so for Evelyn Waugh, who agreed with these younger men no more on this issue than on politics, but who did agree with them to the extent that he even made the house of childhood a central motif in his fiction. We have seen how important the theme of the great and noble house has been in his novels; closely related to it is this second motif of romantic attachment to the period of childhood and youth. Throughout Waugh's novels, devotion to childhood innocence expresses itself in *ingénu* satire and in what may be spoken of as the return-to-the-nursery theme.

Ingénu satire is an ancient and honorable satirical mode, its most notable fictional expression being Voltaire's *Candide*. No doubt Evelyn Waugh's adoption of the *ingénu* satire is in some significant measure a satirical tactic, for the innocent provides the satirist with a particularly effective means of exposing vice and folly. Paul Pennyfeather is, in large part, a kind of dummy. In the scene in which Margot Beste-Chetwynde, seated with Paul in her "game" room, is hiring new "girls" for her South American enterprises, we can see how effectively the technique operates:

> Paul sat in the corner—on a chair made in the shape of an inflated Channel swimmer—enraptured at her business ability. All her vagueness had left her; she sat upright at the table, which was covered with Balmoral tartan, her pen poised over an inkpot, which was set in a stuffed grouse, the very embodiment of the Feminist movement. One by one the girls were shown in.
>
> "Name?" said Margot.
>
> "Pompilia de la Conradine."
>
> "Real name?"
>
> "Bessy Brown."
>
> "Age?"
>
> "Twenty-two."
>
> "Real age?"
>
> "Twenty-two."
>
> "Experience?"
>
> "I was at Mrs. Rosenbaum's, in Jermyn Street, for two years, mum."
>
> "Well, Bessy, I'll see what I can do for you. Why did you leave Mrs. Rosenbaum's?"
>
> "She said her gentlemen liked a change."
>
> "I'll just ask her." Margot took up the telephone, which was held by a boxing glove. "Is that Mrs. Rosenbaum? This is Latin-American Entertainments, Ltd., speaking. Can you tell me about Miss de la Conradine? . . . Oh, that was the reason she left you? Thank you so much! I rather thought that might be it." She rang off. "Sorry, Bessy; nothing for you just at present."

And so the interviews continue, Paul lost in admiration of Margot's administrative efficiency. Then:

> "I say, Margot, there was one thing I couldn't understand. Why was it that the less experience those girls had, the more you seemed to want them? You offered much higher wages to the ones who said they'd never had a job before."
>
> "Did I, darling? I expect it was because I feel so absurdly happy."
>
> At the time this seemed quite a reasonable explanation, but, thinking

the matter over, Paul had to admit to himself that there had been nothing noticeably lighthearted in Margot's conduct of her business.

The advantages of the *ingénu* satire are most amusingly revealed in this passage. Of course, Paul himself is made to seem foolish, but, even more importantly, his innocence provides a sharp contrast to the brazenness of Mrs. Beste-Chetwynde. As have other accomplished practitioners of the mode, Waugh has seized upon the ironic manner of *ingénu* satire to give the reader a means of evaluating the essential object of such satire—not the *naïf* himself but the world which surrounds him. When the innocent becomes involved in action, the possibilities for dramatic irony are multifarious. William Boot, the naïve protagonist of *Scoop,* who has been confused with a novelist, John Boot, is sent much against his will as a special correspondent to cover an incipient civil war in Ishmaelia. Boot proves to be a thoroughly incompetent correspondent and is a perfect reflector of the grubby practices of the other correspondents and reporters, of the falsity of the newspaper world, and of the plotting of Communists who hope to usurp control of the republic. His worldly confreres are tricked into making a trip into the hinterland, but Boot refuses to leave Jacksonburg and, purely by chance, gets the story which proves to be the "scoop," largely on the basis of information provided by Katchen, a young woman who has discovered the advantages of his expense account. So the *naïf* is well suited also to express the irony of events.

The innocent, however, is undoubtedly something more than a satiric tactic; his persistence as a type in Waugh's novels indicates a fundamental orientation toward youthful innocence. This is the quality which characterizes not only Boot and Pennyfeather but also Adam Fenwick-Symes and Nina of *Vile Bodies,* whose "sophistication" about matters of sex is really a mask for inexperience, and Tony Last of

A Handful of Dust. Naïveté is also a characteristic of the later three-dimensional heroes, Charles Ryder and, particularly, Guy Crouchback. Even the Bright Young People, depraved as they sometimes are, carry on with a kind of wide-eyed candor.

Often Waugh's heroes are enamored of childhood. Tony Last has slept in Morgan Le Fay since he left the nursery and maintains in the cherished room "a gallery representative of every phase of his adolescence": pictures of a dreadnought from *Chums* and of boys from his private school; his collections of eggs, butterflies, fossils, and coins; and his books—among them *Bevis, Woodwork at Home, Conjuring for All, The Young Visiters,* and another work about innocence, *Farewell to Arms.* William Boot is also attached to the room of his childhood; he cannot orient himself when he awakens away from home, for he misses the faded wallpaper, the water colors, the books, and the stuffed ferret which greet him every morning at Boot Magna Hall. When he finally escapes from the horrors of the modern world, Boot returns to the nursery where we see him playing dominoes with Nanny Bloggs, who reminds him, as he leaves for dinner, to wash his hands and brush his hair. Apparently they order things better in the nursery.

The games of childhood are important in Waugh's novels also: dominoes, Halma, Happy Families, Animal Snap—all provide convenient retreats for his characters. Basil Seal steals, cheats, lies, lives off one woman and betrays her with others, but when he visits Alastair and Sonia Trumpington, they play, after a dinner enjoyed by all sitting together in one bed, Happy Families:

> "Have you got Miss Chipps, the Carpenter's daughter."
>
> "*Not at home* but have *you* got Mr. Chipps the Carpenter? *Thank you and* Mrs. Chipps the Carpenter's wife. . . ."

Then when Basil returns from Azania where he participated in a feast at which the main dish happened to be his mistress, he visits the Trumpingtons, once again plays Happy Families, and leaves with them for a new cocktail club.

Ten years later, in *Put Out More Flags,* as England mobilizes for war, Basil and his sister Barbara are still paying visits to the nursery. When Barbara cries because the butler, harried by evacuees from the London slums, threatens to leave, Basil teases her:

> "Babs, you're blubbing."
>
> "Who wouldn't?" said Barbara, pulling out a handkerchief and weeping in earnest. "I ask you, who wouldn't?"
>
> "Don't be a chump," said Basil relapsing, as he often did with Barbara, into the language of the schoolroom. "I'll fix it for you."
>
> "Swank. Chump yourself. Double chump."
>
> "Double chump with knobs on."
>
> "Darling Basil, it is nice to have you back. I do believe if anyone could fix it, you could."
>
> "Freddy couldn't, could he?"
>
> "Freddy isn't here."
>
> "I'm cleverer than Freddy. Babs, say I'm cleverer than Freddy."
>
> "I'm cleverer than Freddy. Sucks to you."
>
> "Babs, say you love me more than Freddy."
>
> "You love me more than Freddy. Double sucks."
>
> "Say I, Barbara, love you, Basil, more than him, Freddy."
>
> "I won't. I don't. . . . Beast, you're hurting."
>
> "Say it."
>
> "Basil, stop at once or I shall call Miss Penfold."
>
> They were back twenty years, in the schoolroom again.

Little wonder that the slum child who finds them scuffling on the sofa imagines that they are "Aving a lark," but, knowing as she is, she cannot comprehend their ingenuousness. Even the rogue-hero possesses the quality of innocence and is made to appear sympathetic by his return to the nursery.

Donat O'Donnell, writing of a group of Catholic writers—François Mauriac, Georges Bernanos, Graham Greene, Sean O'Faolain, Evelyn Waugh, Charles Peguy, Paul Claudel, and Leon Bloy—finds that they all to a remarkable degree turn backward nostalgically to the period of childhood. In Evelyn

Waugh, in particular, he finds a "preoccupation with youth."[2] An even severer critic of the pervasive motifs of innocence and the nursery is D. S. Savage, who argues that Waugh "reveals the predicament of immaturity." Waugh is, according to this critic, "the brilliant undergraduate who has difficulty in growing up" and consequently regards things through "the mists of sentiment exhaled from a childish or adolescent innocence."[3] We may well consider the criticism that the two writers make: Waugh sentimentalizes childhood and youth, and, in dealing with them through the two motifs discussed here, loses satirical detachment.

To a degree both of these criticisms would seem to be valid. After all, William Boot's return to the nursery is not an adequate answer to the problems the modern world has thrust upon him; and yet this escape from maturity is certainly to be taken as a superior alternative to his experiences "outside." To make this observation is not, of course, to argue that disengagement from violence is sentimental, but only that a flight to the nursery is. Although the games of Basil and Barbara are meant to be engaging—indeed, reveal Basil in practically his only meaningful relationship with another person—is there not something to be said for the slum girl's reaction to them? They are somehow unwholesome, particularly for a man and woman nearing middle age.

In *Brideshead Revisited* the consequences of this romantic attachment to youth are more complicated. Sebastian, who is in love with his childhood and whose character is brilliantly realized in the earlier half of the novel, is captivating indeed:

> . . . he was the most conspicuous man of the year by reason of his beauty, which was arresting, and his eccentricities of behavior which seemed to know no bounds. My first sight of him was as he passed the door of Germer's, and, on that occasion, I was less struck by his looks than by the fact that he was carrying a large Teddy-bear.
>
> "That," said the barber, as I took his chair, "was Lord Sebastian Flyte. A most amusing young gentleman."
>
> "Apparently," I said coldly.

"The Marquis of Marchmain's second boy. His brother, the Earl of Brideshead, went down last term. Now he was very different, a very quiet gentleman. . . . What do you suppose Lord Sebastian wanted? A hair brush for his Teddy-bear; it had to have very stiff bristles, *not* as Lord Sebastian said, to brush him with, but to threaten him with a spanking when he was sulky. He bought a very nice one with an ivory back and he's having 'Aloysius' engraved on it—that's the bear's name." The man, who, in his time, had had ample chance to tire of undergraduate fantasy, was plainly captivated by him.

When Sebastian first conducts Charles Ryder to Brideshead, he comes not to meet the family but, on a visit often repeated, to his nanny in the nursery. Years later Ryder lyrically recalls the charms of youth, as he speaks with great feeling of the "home-sickness for nursery morality" which characterized the Oxford years. Still, Sebastian's desire that it be "like this always—always summer, always alone, the fruit always ripe, and Aloysius always in a good temper" is seen to be fatal. His love for his own childhood—for his teddy-bear and his nanny—and his inability to confront the world outside the nursery almost destroy him. Yet despite this awareness of the possible destructiveness of idealizing innocence and youth, Waugh, himself prone to such idealization, sets out so fully and affectionately to evoke this period in the lives of Sebastian and Ryder that he creates a serious structural defect in the novel.

Men at Arms, the first of three novels dealing with the war career of Guy Crouchback, is Waugh's most satisfactory and complex exploration of the two motifs I have been considering. Crouchback, who has obvious links to the earlier and younger men of Waugh's novels, is not the one-dimensional earlier type but a fully developed character. As the novel opens he welcomes the outbreak of war with Germany, since it seems to give some purpose to his life. Diffident, withdrawn, living an essentially sterile life—in isolation in Italy—Crouchback is a man with a wound from which he has been unable to recover: he had been cuckolded seven years before by the smart young woman who was his wife. Crouchback is incapacitated in other respects, too, for he is cut off from others not only by his diffidence but by a certain spiritual dryness. Unloved by his household and by the inhabitants of the town in which he lives, he is friendless and feels himself at odds even with his fellow communicants of the Roman Catholic church. When he meets Major Tickeridge, the Halberdier officer who gains an entry into the corps for him, Guy can manage only "an embarrassed grunt" to the Major's cheerful "Here's how" over pink gin.

But as a prospective officer in the ancient and honored Corps of Halberdiers, he finds himself in a house where a generation of officers and gentlemen have resided, and he begins his passionate love affair with the army. Experiencing for the first time association with his fellows and friendship with a broadly comic figure called Apthorpe, Guy feels that he is enjoying "something he had missed in boyhood, a happy adolescence." The Halberdiers offer Crouchback many of the values which the novelist himself passionately admires: tradition, continuity, order, ritual. In the men and officers, in the training, in the formal dinners followed by port and snuff, Guy finds a kind of fulfillment he has not known before. The Christmas dinner to which he proudly brings his nephew is "one simple sublime delight." The toast to the Grand-Duchess Elena of Russia; the ritualistic passing of the horn of snuff; the silver goblets "brimming with champagne"—all these seem to complete the romantic dreams of adolescence. And finally the games of youth take place:

> Presently the adjutant started a game of football with a waste-paper basket. They changed from soccer to rugger. Leonard had the basket. He was tackled and brought down. All the young officers began to leap on the struggling bodies. Apthorpe leapt. Guy leapt. Others leapt on them. Guy was conscious of a wrench in the knee; then the wind was knocked out of him and he lay momentarily paralyzed. Dusty, laughing, sweating, panting, they disentangled themselves and got to their feet. Guy felt a remote but serious pain in his knee.

The next morning, of course, Guy's knee is badly swollen, and he is unable to walk.

The satire is handled here with marvelous delicacy, for Waugh manages to suggest both the attractiveness and the illusoriness of everything that Guy has committed himself to, at the same time that he ridicules with restraint and poise Crouchback's failure to recognize his illusions. Guy, who does not comprehend the deflating significance of his leg injury, believes that he is about to experience "the full consummation of his love for the Royal Corps of Halberdiers." On leave in London he even finds himself able to exchange an easy "Cheerio" or "Here's how" at Bellamy's bar. Then, too, Guy has met Colonel Ritchie-Hook, "the great Halberdier *enfant terrible* of the first World War," who, it has been noted, has certain obvious resemblances to Captain Hook of *Peter Pan*.[4] Ritchie-Hook seems to return Guy to public school; he is devoted to practical jokes, so much so that "For this remarkable warrior the image of war was not hunting or shooting; it was the wet sponge on the door, the hedgehog in the bed."

The return to boyhood seems complete when the movement orders appear, and Guy finds that he has been stationed for further training at the Kut-al-Imara House, a former boys' school. Here Guy and his fellows move into the boys' quarters, the married men who live out are known as "dayboys," the school bell rings to summon the trainees to duty, and the "preparatory school way of life" is "completely recreated." The preparatory school way of life becomes even more real when Ritchie-Hook arrives to take over the training, which has not gone well. This extraordinary gentleman's first move, after dressing the men down, is to institute a game of Housey-housey, a "noisy sport," which seems to be an elaborate version of Beano. The sports and games continue, in the novel's most boisterous sequence, as Ritchie-Hook wages war on

Apthorpe and his "thunderbox." Apthorpe, who does not quite trust the sanitary conditions of the latrine, is extremely proud of a chemical toilet he has concealed on the grounds of Kut-al-Imara. To his outrage, he discovers that someone is using it; at first suspecting Crouchback, he is appalled to discover that Ritchie-Hook is his antagonist. A series of skirmishes follows, all of which Apthorpe loses: first the shed in which he has concealed the box is marked off bounds; later he is beaned by a falling plant pot; finally he is blown up by a booby trap—all devices of the Colonel.

By the end of the training period, "the chimes" of Guy's boyhood peal for him; he feels he has now at last begun to live the adventures of Captain Truslove, whose deeds had excited the top-forms when the housemaster read to them. But terrible disappointments befall him. At the end of the course Guy is not given a company; the evacuation of Dunkirk seems anything but Truslove-like; months of chaos, rumors, and orders follow before Guy embarks with a force for a landing at Dakar in French West Africa. When the landing is canceled, Ritchie-Hook decides upon a little "unofficial fun." Guy is to take a small landing party onto the beach, ostensibly to boost morale. "This was true Truslove-style," Guy reflects. Unknown to him, however, Ritchie-Hook joins the party, face blackened against discovery, only to return with the head of a native sentry, whom he has decapitated in sporting fashion, and with a wound that brings the entire unauthorized escapade to the attention of superior officers. Guy, who has acted at the command of his superior, learns that the expedition has earned him not the reward he deserves but a black mark on his record, one that will follow him until the end of his service. He loses his command and is ordered back to England. To dispel further the illusion of Guy's return to the fantasies of adolescence, Apthorpe, sick of a fever, dies after polishing off a bottle of liquor Guy smuggled in to him at the company's behest. At the novel's close, Guy's brigadier informs him that, while he will be spared a court-martial, he will be posted out of the brigade as soon as the inquiry is over in England. Though unashamed and free of guilt, Crouchback is overwhelmed by "a trembling, hopeless sense of disaster."

As Guy is flown to England, his comrades discuss his fate. "Pity he made an ass of himself," one comments. "Already the Second Battalion of the Halberdiers spoke of Guy in the past tense. He had momentarily been of them; now he was an alien." So Guy is once again an exile from his fellows, and the retreat into the romantic fantasies of childhood has been shattered by reality. The striking fact about this artful satire is that Waugh creates in Ritchie-Hook—with his hook, monocle, extraordinary grin, and talk of "biffing" the enemy—a figure, at once romantic and comic, who embodies a quixotic heroism the author obviously respects. At the same time, however, Waugh is able to discern the limitations of that romantic attachment to childhood for which he has been criticized. Consequently, *Men at Arms* is both moving and profoundly ironic.

CHAPTER V

Antiheroes and Victims

IT HAS often been observed that one of the striking phenomena in the history of the novel during the nineteenth and twentieth centuries has been the disappearance of the traditional hero, characterized by a certain nobility and vitality of spirit, and the appearance of an antiheroic type. Mario Praz explains the eclipse of the hero in the Victorian novel in terms of the triumph of bourgeois morality and sentimentality. A number of other explanations might be offered: the disruption of Western civilization, the waning of religion, political revolution, mass production, industrialism, Darwinism, naturalism, the impact of scientific skepticism. The fact is that such phenomena can seldom be easily traced to single forces, and probably all of these developments have influenced the conception of man as he is depicted in modern fiction.

In any case, Sean O'Faolain seems to make a reasonable observation when he states that the "Hero in our time has been replaced by what, for want of a better word, we have come to call the anti-hero." In *The Vanishing Hero* O'Faolain observes that the antiheroic figure in the works of a number of modern novelists, among whom he includes Evelyn Waugh, is "always presented as groping, puzzled, cross, mocking, frustrated, and isolated," and "Whatever he is, weak or brave, brainy or bewildered, his one abiding characteristic is that, like his author-creator, he is never able to see any Pattern in life and rarely its Destination."[1]

More particularly, the antihero as he appears in Waugh's satires is, with the exception of Basil Seal, a passive figure. He is the man to whom things happen; and the things that happen to him often do so without rhyme or reason, because the world he inhabits is, as O'Faolain says, one without "pattern." Paul Pennyfeather, Adam Fenwick-Symes, William Boot, and Tony Last are all such figures. No doubt it is possible to explain the passivity of the Waugh heroes and the unfortunate predicaments in which they find themselves partly in terms of the strategy of *ingénu* satire. Extreme and unmerited misfortune would seem to have been a concomitant of the mode since Candide was first kicked in the seat of the pants by Baron Thunder-ten-Tronckh. But we must note again that the persistence of this type in the novels—from Pennyfeather right down to his modification in Charles Ryder and Guy Crouchback—indicates that the antihero is something more than a satirical tactic, and amounts to a comment on the nature of man in contemporary society, and particularly on the condition of man during the twenties and thirties of this century when the disorder of social and moral values was assailing Pennyfeather, Symes, Boot, and Last.

At one point in *Decline and Fall,* Waugh pauses to observe that Pennyfeather "would never have made a hero, and the only interest about him arises from the unusual series of events of which his shadow was witness." Waugh might as well have spoken of the events to which his shadow was subjected, for such is the nature of Pennyfeather's experience. When the novel opens Paul is a serious, moderate, and dull young Oxonian. At his college one evening he has the misfortune to meet members of the Bollinger Club who have departed from their gathering in some disorder and considerable drunkenness. These gentlemen remove Pennyfeather's trousers. "Next morning there was a lovely College meeting" at which the Bollinger pranksters were heavily fined and Pennyfeather, who, according to the Junior Dean, had no money, was sent down for indecent behavior. Pennyfeather does not leave, however, until the Domestic Bursar has extracted a fine for "two slight burns" in his room and the Junior Dean has congratulated him on discovering his unfitness for the priesthood. " 'God damn and blast them all to hell,' said Paul meekly to himself as he drove to the station, and then he felt rather ashamed, because he rarely swore." These events establish the nature of Pennyfeather's experience, for the rest of the novel deals with the things that happen to him or are done to him in a confusing world.

Similarly, William Boot is torn away from the blissful seclusion of Boot Magna Hall (which corresponds to Pennyfeather's Oxford) and his weekly wildlife column "Lush Places"; he is forced to go to Ishmaelia as a reporter for the *Daily Beast;* and then fixed upon by Katchen, a young lady who finds him so amenable that at one point she suggests that she might marry him so as to divorce him later and gain citizenship for her German lover.

The fates of Adam Fenwick-Symes and of Tony Last are more serious; neither of these is able to return to such security as Oxford or Boot Magna Hall offers. Indeed, these two antiheroes might more properly be described as victims. Returning from France with a number of books and the manuscript of an autobiography on which he has already had an advance, Adam has some trouble with the Customs:

"You can take these books on architecture and the dictionary, and I don't mind stretching a point for once and letting you have the history books too. But this book on Economics comes under Subversive Propaganda. That you leaves behind. And this here *Purgatorio* doesn't look right to me, so that stays behind. . . . But as for this autobiography, that's just downright dirt, and we burns that straight away, see."

Consequently, Adam has to postpone his marriage and accept a new contract with his publisher, a contract that provides no royalty on the first two thousand copies, "then a royalty of two and a half per cent., rising to five per cent. on the tenth thousand." In addition, the publisher retains "serial, cinema, dramatic, American, colonial and translation rights" and holds an option on Adam's next twelve books on the same terms.

Just as arbitrary and illogical are the events that place an elusive fortune in his hands. A casual exchange with another guest at Lottie Crump's hotel, where the champagne constantly flows, wins him a thousand pounds. Another casual exchange puts the money in the hands of a drunken major, who offers to place it on a horse for him. The appearance and disappearance of the major, whose name Adam never learns and with whom he is never able to establish contact at an appropriate moment to obtain the fortune he has won on the bet, indicate the incoherence of the life the Bright Young People lead, the purely fortuitous nature of events, and Adam's incapacity for controlled action. In the "Happy Ending" with which the novel closes, Adam is found on "the biggest battlefield in the history of the world," surrounded by "unrelieved desolation"; there Adam is threatened by a man with a liquid-fire projector who turns out to be his major, now a general. The general offers him his thirty-five thousand pounds, by then worth the price of a couple of drinks and a newspaper. As the sounds of the battle, "like a circling typhoon," return, the reader can feel little optimism about the fate of Adam Fenwick-Symes.

Tony Last is also victimized by the chaotic nature of his society and by the absurd. Willing to provide an adequate support for Brenda, who has cuckolded him, he rebels when he is expected to sell his family home, Hetton, to provide a substantial income for both Brenda and her lover. But, characteristically, he permits himself to be talked into an expedition to the interior of Venezuela in search of a fabled city with an inexperienced explorer, Dr. Messenger, who is a "crook doctor" according to the more worldly Jock de Menzies. After the bearers have deserted and Dr. Messenger has drowned, Tony, nearly dead from malaria, stumbles into a native village fathered (quite literally) by Mr. Todd, the less than half-civilized natural son of a Barbadian missionary. Here Tony is nursed back to health. But his final victimization is probably the most absurd and horrifying that Evelyn Waugh's imagination has conceived. When a search party arrives, Tony, drugged by Todd, is assumed dead; virtually imprisoned by his host, he is forced to read aloud the works of Charles Dickens, over and over, over and over again.

The antihero who emerged during the second stage of Waugh's career was Basil Seal, a victimizer who parallels the rogues of Anthony Powell's *Agents and Patients,* the "Snooty" Baronet of Wyndham Lewis, and Anthony Farrant of Graham Greene's *England Made Me.* Farrant, for example, is a charming yet somewhat battered and debauched young man who has failed in everything that he has tried, who has been prepared by his middle-class upbringing for nothing, and who has been corrupted by the false standards of a second-rate public school background. Although Farrant has lived off his charm, exploited women, victimized others whenever possible, he is thoroughly weak and incapable of any meaningful action; his most intense relationship, with his sister, has incestuous overtones.

The parallel with Basil Seal is striking, except that Basil is many steps higher on the social scale than Farrant. Surely the appearance of two such similar figures—one in a melodrama, the other in a satire—indicates that both novelists have observed a common type of their times. In fact, the problem of both Farrant and Basil is that their society has not provided them with any means of expressing whatever capacity they do have. However, striking differences exist between the two portraits. Greene regards Farrant as pitiful and damned; Waugh is delighted with Basil Seal, whatever his crimes.

Whereas Greene suggests that Anthony Farrant's society has failed him by filling his head with base illusions about the end and conduct of life, Basil Seal's career seems to imply that his society is too mean and petty for such a swashbuckler. Finally, Greene's Anthony Farrant is seedy and wretched; Basil Seal, who certainly finds himself in enough seedy and wretched situations, has qualities of swank, swagger, and pluck that somehow lift him above the seediness.

When we first encounter him in *Black Mischief,* Basil wakes up on the sofa of a totally strange flat, after a four day "racket" precipitated by the forced withdrawal of his candidacy for Parliament. A few hours later, he decides that he will go to Azania, where the Emperor, a slight acquaintance of his at Oxford, is in trouble. Seal, therefore, crashes a party at Margot Metroland's place. His mission—to obtain money from his sister, who would give it but is unable, and employment from Lord Monomark, who disdains and dismisses him—is entirely without success but not without comment from the debutantes:

> He stood in the doorway, a glass of whiskey in one hand, looking insolently round the room, his hand back, chin forward, shoulders rounded, dark hair over his forehead, contemptuous grey eyes over grey pouches, a proud rather childish mouth, a scar on one cheek.
>
> "My word, he is a corker," remarked one of the girls.

The childish pout on Basil's mouth cannot be overlooked, for it associates him with the naïve types of the earlier satires. In Basil, however, the innocence of immaturity leads to complete amorality and to the irresponsible cruelty which permits him to victimize others. So he can first steal an emerald necklace from his mother, without hesitation or sense of guilt, and then accept a sizable check, to finance his expedition to Azania, from his mistress, whom he has been treating rather badly. He knows that "Every year or so there's one place on the globe worth going to where things are happening," and he is determined to go to Azania. Unfortunately, Azania proves to be as much of a fizzle as London, and when Basil appears ten years later in *Put Out More Flags* he is still looking for the proper sphere in which to exercise his capabilities.

Alas, Basil does not immediately fulfill his sister's hope that he will find his proper, heroic role in the war; instead he spends part of the first year of the war exercising his talents as a victimizer. In his capacity of billeting officer, he uses three atrocious slum children to swindle the householders around his sister's country estate: these children are so incredibly destructive and vile that Basil's victims are willing to pay for their removal.

Finally Basil wangles the rank of second lieutenant on the General Service List and a position with the Director of Internal Security. Seeking a promotion, he weaves a web around Ambrose Silk—Jewish, homosexual, aesthetic associate of left-wing poets and party members during the thirties. Basil turns Ambrose in as a Fascist; Ambrose's new and nonpolitical magazine *The Ivory Tower,* wherein appears his account of his tragic love affair with a young storm trooper (edited at Basil's insistence in such a way that it reads like "the triumphant paean of Hitler young") provides excellent evidence against him. But when credit for the affair seems to go not so much to Basil as to his superior, and when he, for the first time in his career, feels some few, slight qualms, Basil helps Ambrose flee to Ireland, then moves into his apartment and even into his expensive underwear. At the conclusion of the novel, caught up in the enthusiasm of the Churchillian renaissance, Basil leaves the war office and joins a special *corps d'élite.* Many readers have been somewhat unconvinced by Basil's noble and patriotic gesture; but, in fact, it is consistent with the implication that Basil has always needed such a calling.

Nigel Dennis has advanced the theory, with respect to this clash between the victimizer and the victim, that *Put Out More Flags* is "more than a parable of war" and that the conflict between the aesthete and the man of action is Waugh's own conflict.[2] The extreme polarization in this novel of the passive figure and the active one marks an important stage in the satirist's career. Ambrose Silk is made to seem thoroughly ridiculous in a way that the earlier victim antiheroes never were; though there is some pathos in the characterization, he is essentially the ludicrous figure of fun at whom lounging soldiers make rude noises. Not only is Ambrose driven into exile at the novel's end, but another victim-figure, Cedric Lyne, the cuckolded husband of Basil's mistress who has devoted his life to the collection of grottoes, is killed in the early days of the war. (Among later characters, only Major Hound of *Officers and Gentlemen* can be classified as pure "victim," and he is a subordinate character, unsympathetically handled.) The exile of Ambrose and the death of Lyne mark the disappearance of the entirely passive antihero from Waugh's fiction, as the transformation of Basil Seal into a commando marks the displacement of the rogue-hero.

The heroes of *Brideshead Revisited* and of *Men at Arms, Officers and Gentlemen,* and *Unconditional Surrender* have some of the characteristics of the victim, but Charles Ryder has certain qualities which make one reluctant to classify him as an antihero, and Guy Crouchback is Waugh's first real hero. Both of these men have been victimized by women; like Adam Fenwick-Symes and Tony Last and Cedric Lyne, they have been betrayed. Both men inhabit hostile worlds. Ryder, an architectural painter, has devoted his life to recording the passing of great houses; and, cruelly enough, he is often commissioned to paint them just before their demolition. When we see him in the prologue and epilogue to *Brideshead,* his intense hostility to the "ice age" in which he lives is clearly apparent. Crouchback closely resembles him, has welcomed the Second World War as an opportunity, since Russia and Germany have made their infamous pact, to fight the "Modern Age." His experience in the war is, however, entirely disillusioning, and he finds himself witnessing the further decay of social and moral values. Ryder loses his dearest friend, Sebastian; his wife, Celia; his love, Julia. Crouchback loses his wife; his friend, Ivor Claire, who deserts his post; his love, the army. Idealizing his corps, he is disillusioned and held responsible for actions that he could not have controlled; idealizing his country's heroic traditions, he is disenchanted by her ignominious withdrawal from Crete and her alliance with Russia. Both men are pessimistic to an extreme degree about the course their nation seems to be taking, a departure, as it seems to them, from the traditions of the past to which they are devoted.

And yet Ryder and Crouchback possess capacities which set them apart from a victim and antihero such as Tony Last. Their courage, their stoic and silent endurance of suffering, their capacity for avoiding despair—all these go back to their religious commitment to Roman Catholicism. They suffer, but they are sustained by the knowledge that the sanctuary lamp burns at Brideshead and Broome. Moreover, Guy Crouchback attains a degree of self-knowledge that is unequaled in any other of Waugh's central characters. Learning that honor cannot be achieved through violence and that only through charity may the individual hope to redeem the times, he seeks (and does not entirely fail) to bring some personal order into the chaos of social and political upheaval. In effect, then, while Catholicism has not altered Evelyn Waugh's rejection of the time in which he lives, it has emerged gradually in his novels as a positive answer to the plight of the individual, whom Waugh had earlier seen as entirely vulnerable to social and moral disintegration.

Part Three

THE SATIRICAL REBELLION

CHAPTER VI

Waugh and the Satirical Speculum

In "Fan-fare," an essay written after *Brideshead Revisited,* Evelyn Waugh insisted that his novels were not satirical. He reasoned that satire is "a matter of period" and that "it flourishes in a stable society and presupposes homogeneous moral standards." Satire, he went on, "exposes polite cruelty and folly by exaggerating them" and "seeks to produce shame." None of this has any place, he ruefully concluded, "in the Century of the Common Man when vice no longer pays lip service to virtue."[1] At the basis of these statements, of course, is the assumption that we live in a period when homogeneous and fixed standards do not exist and in which, consequently, satire is impossible.

These views of Evelyn Waugh are both instructive and misleading. To begin with, we must question his assumption that satire is only written during periods of social stability when certain common and widely-shared values are in existence. Satire is often written under such conditions, the eighteenth century being the most notable example. Nevertheless, it is just as possible that satire may be written during periods of instability, when the artist feels that traditional or peculiarly personal values are challenged. Aristophanes and Juvenal certainly did not regard their own times as stable ones, and probably one of the impulses behind their satires is resentment at the absence of homogeneous values. Byron is another satirist who writes not from the point of view of values accepted by his society but from outside, from values which he regards as personal. It is clear that the satirical novelists of our times belong to his class—Norman Douglas, Ronald Firbank, Aldous Huxley, Wyndham Lewis, and even Waugh, with his commitment to the oldest of the churches—writing from values which are not commonly held by their fellows.

Waugh's observations are misleading in another sense, for they seem to suggest that cruelty, folly, and exaggeration have no place in his fiction. But even a casual reader must know that they do. Nevertheless, the comments are also instructive, for when a man tells us that shamelessness is one of the central characteristics of his time and when he speaks with scorn of his age as "the Century of the Common Man," we know that he has the satirical sensibility: he is, in short, both angry and ironic. And even granting that the twentieth century is not apt to be described as a period of homogeneous value and common belief, Waugh overstates the case; we are, after all, not so barbarized that we are unable to respond to traditional appeals to reason and order. And we do laugh, or suffer, when Waugh, in common with other satirists, exposes men to ridicule by revealing the differences between things—between what the reader ordinarily assumes life to be and what the novelist has seen it to be, between our knowledge of reality and the writer's exaggeration of some aspect of life, between the words of man and his deeds, between his deeds and his thoughts.

Undoubtedly, however, the question of Waugh's satirical perspective is a perplexing one. In his Jungian study of Waugh, Frederic J. Stopp consistently and frequently refers to Waugh as a satirist and to the novels as satires. Yet at one point he accedes to Waugh's disclaimer of satirical intention, reasoning that in the early novels Waugh did not work from a stable moral point of view. Then, however, he argues that Waugh created a fantasy world "with moral implications"; next he asserts that the general implications of Waugh's novels are moral but that specific fates to which the characters are subjected are governed by fantasy. Finally, coming full circle, he indicates that even the fanciful fates are "poetically just."[2] An examination of Evelyn Waugh's techniques and a careful consideration of the evolution of his point of view should demonstrate not only why the satires have provoked such contradictory observations as these, but also that the novels are pervaded by the spirit of satire.

To begin with, Evelyn Waugh's way of seeing things is undeniably satirical. He revels in what William Hazlitt, defining satire, spoke of as a nice and subtle awareness of differences. Throughout his career, particularly in his earlier works, Waugh has delighted in startling, even shocking, incongruities. Sean O'Faolain pointed out Waugh's mastery of the "eclectic adjective,"[3] and a mere glance through the novels reveals Waugh's extraordinary sense of adjectival incongruity. When Paul Pennyfeather was sent down from Oxford, we learn that "there was a lovely College meeting." In the same work we find such lines as this: "Ten men of revolting appearance were approaching from the drive," and, a clear echo of Ronald Firbank, "Who's that dear, dim, drunk little man?" A casual skimming of *Vile Bodies* turns up, "They spent a jolly morning strapping each other's tummies," and a delighted, if perverse, description of Archie Schwartz as "The *most* bogus man."

Waugh's awareness of the comic possibilities of incongruity in language is not confined to the adjective. Consider the sentence, "Two days later Beste-Chetwynde pulled out the *vox humana* and played *Pop Goes the Weasel.*" Or, the one in which the publisher Lord Monomark, not knowing of his columnist Balcairn's suicide, promises that, "I'll raise him tomorrow first thing." Innumerable sentences of this sort further suggest Waugh's command of the explosive possibility of diction. While such purely verbal fun became less obtrusive as Waugh developed his own strengths and grew less dependent on the Firbank manner, it is an element which has never entirely disappeared from his work. Moreover, Waugh's novels abound in the casually noted ironic detail which suddenly bursts in our consciousness, revealing just how mad the world is. For example: "With Asiatic resignation Father Rothschild S. J. put down his suitcase in the corner of the bar and went on deck." And, of that suitcase we learn that "It contained some rudimentary underclothes, six important new books in six languages, a false beard and a school atlas and gazetteer heavily annotated."

Perhaps experience, by its very nature, has thrust itself upon Evelyn Waugh as incongruous and absurd. Commenting on the characterizations of his novels, Waugh has written, "Men and women as I see them would not be credible if . . . literally transcribed."[4] In effect, then, he must see human beings in terms of some distortion or exaggeration of what he regards as the credible or of what he thinks *we* would regard as credible. From this particular view he selects his details, for he reports of the character Grimes in *Decline and Fall* that, "had I written anything like a full account of his iniquities, my publishers and I would have been in the police court."* Given the finished portrait of the novel, which is certainly grotesque, we must conclude that Evelyn Waugh's way of seeing people, then of selecting from that vision, is just as ineluctably satirical as his manner of using language or responding to situation.

* Evelyn Waugh, "Fan-fare," *Life* (April 8, 1946), p. 56. The fuller account of "Grimes" that Waugh gives in the first volume of his autobiography, *A Little Learning* (1964), is extraordinary, indeed. Even in this nonfictional treatment, however, Waugh's sense of "Grimes," who might have been rendered as a pathetic victim of aberrant appetites, is that of the satirist. One wonders, for instance, what Graham Greene would have noticed about "Grimes"; and one can imagine how differently Greene would have treated him in a novel.

The characters within the novels fall into three groups. One group is that of the *ingénus* or *naïfs,* who are usually the central characters—Pennyfeather, Fenwick-Symes, Boot, for instance. Another group is composed of certain subsidiary, though important figures, nearly always of the upper classes, closely associated with the "heroes." Such characters as Margot Beste-Chetwynde and Peter Pastmaster, the Bright Young People, Sonia and Alastair Trumpington, Barbara Seal, Prudence Courtenay, Brenda Last, John Beaver, Jock de Menzies, Angela Lyne, Sebastian and Julia Marchmain, Virginia Troy, Tommy Blackhouse, and Ivor Claire belong to this set. Waugh uses understatement to characterize both of these groups. He gives some incisive, concrete details to suggest their characters; then dialogue and action are allowed to stand by themselves.

Finally, there is a large group of characters who belong to the sphere of grotesque satire: Grimes, Prendergast, Philbrick, Mrs. Melrose-Ape, Father Rothschild, Lord Metroland, Mr. Youkoumian, Seth, Sir Samson Courtenay, Mr. Baldwin, Ambrose Silk, the Connolly children, Anthony Blanche, Aimée Thanatogenos, Mr. Joyboy, Apthorpe, Ritchie-Hook, Trimmer, Major Hound, Ludovic, and others. There are significant exceptions to the rule, but for the most part these characters belong either to the "lower orders," to alien races and peoples, or to a social group which somehow fails to be of the aristocracy. Some of these grotesques are given single, exaggerated characteristics which "tag" them; they are then developed through repetition with variation. For example, Mr. Youkoumian, the Armenian trader in *Black Mischief,* is perhaps the quintessential "tagged" grotesque. Ever the same, infinitely various, he is always at some shady business venture—selling places on his escape yacht, manufacturing "champagne," running a store, keeping a hotel, selling boots to the army. Other grotesques, such as Ambrose Silk, the monstrous Connolly children, or Apthorpe, though they also have central governing characteristics, are built up through minuteness of detail. Played off against the understated characters of Waugh's ironic mode, these grotesques, who shock as often as they amuse, are one proof of the fertility of Waugh's satiric imagination.

It has been observed that "The tendency of satirical novelists is to progress from burlesque to irony of manner and finally to dramatic irony in which follies and vices speak for themselves without assistance."[5] Evelyn Waugh's development is rather more complex than this. *In toto* his work is marked by detachment, and he exploits the less direct satirical techniques of irony of manner and dramatic irony. In Aldous Huxley's satires, and also in Wyndham Lewis', one finds more pronounced burlesque elements and more direct invective, a mode which Waugh has almost entirely eschewed. Nevertheless, the existence of the grotesques in his novels indicates a persistent strain of something akin to low burlesque. From time to time, elements of the mock-heroic and of parody also enter his work. For example, Grimes is a broadly comic figure, verging on the mock heroic. This element finally becomes pronounced at the moment of the final disappearance of the "old Harrovian," who vanishes in chains from Egdon Heath:

> Grimes, Paul at last realized, was of the immortals. He was a life force. Sentenced to death in Flanders, he popped up in Wales; drowned in Wales, he emerged in South America; engulfed in the dark mystery of Egdon Mire, he would rise again somewhere at sometime, shaking from his limbs the musty integuments of the tomb. Surely he had followed in the Bacchic train of distant Arcady, and played on the reeds of myth by forgotten streams, and taught the childish satyrs the art of love? Had he not suffered unscathed the fearful dooms of all the offended gods of all the histories, fire, brimstone, and yawning earthquakes, plague and pestilence? Had he not stood, like the Pompeian sentry, while the Citadels of the Plain fell to ruin about his ears? Had he not, like some greasecaked Channel swimmer, breasted the waves of the Deluge? Had he not moved unseen when darkness covered the waters?

Waugh also occasionally permits himself a parody of attitudes which strike him as absurd, and there is an element of racial snobbery which prompts him to turn this technique against Negroes. Here is an impassioned speech, savoring of the rhetoric of revivalism, delivered by Chokey, Mrs. Beste-Chetwynde's lover:

> "You folks all think the coloured man hasn't got a soul. Anything's good enough for the poor coloured man. Beat him; put him in chains; load him with burdens. . . . But all the time that poor coloured man has a soul the same as you have. Don't he breathe the same as you? Don't he love Shakespeare and cathedrals and paintings of the old masters same as you? Isn't he just asking for your love and help to raise him from the servitude into which your forefathers plunged him? O, say, white folks, why don't you stretch out a helping hand to the poor coloured man, that's as good as you are, if you'll only let him be?"

The same kind of parodic treatment is given to the Consul-General of Ishmaelia, whose office sports the hammer and sickle and who spouts, in a strangely garbled way, the doctrines of "that great Negro Karl Marx." "Who built the Pyramids?" he cries, finally pausing long enough to wipe "the line of froth" from his mouth. "Who invented the circulation of the blood? . . . Africa for the African worker, Europe for the African worker, Asia, Oceania, America, Arctic and Antarctic for the African worker." Mock-heroic and parodic elements enter into the representation of Seth, "Emperor of Azania, Chief of the Chiefs of the Sakuyu, Lord of Wanda and Tyrant of the Seas, Bachelor of the Arts of Oxford University," who likes to see himself, though surrounded by barbarism and decay, in the forefront rank of Progress. "I have read modern books—Shaw, Arlen, Priestley," he insists. "I am the New Age. I am the Future."

Elements of high and low burlesque are even pronounced in the late novels. In *Men at Arms,* for instance, the "schoolboy" motif burlesques Guy Crouchback's infatuation with the Halberdiers while references to the hero of his childhood reading, Captain Truslove, mock his idealization of his role in the war. The mock-heroic note is sounded also in the characterization and treatment of Apthorpe, the three books of the novel being *Apthorpe Gloriosus, Apthorpe Furibundus,* and *Apthorpe Immolatus.* At crucial moments in Apthorpe's career, surely Waugh's supreme excursion into the "bogus," the satirist is apt to assume the mock-heroic tone. "It was a moment of heightened emotion; an historic moment," he writes; and, parodying Andrew Marvell's lines on Charles I, "He nothing common did or mean on their morning of departure." In *Officers and Gentlemen,* which is three-dimensional in characterization and more "credible" in plot than the earlier works, as are the major works since *Brideshead,* Waugh comes nearer to invective than one expects of him in his practice of satire, particularly in his treatment of Trimmer, a cowardly former hairdresser boomed as a hero; three American reporters—Scab Dunz, Bum Schlum, and Joe Mulligan—drunken, dirty, and ignorant all; and Major Hound, a craven regular officer who represents England's failure on Crete. The portraits of Major Hound and Trimmer, which are the fullest of this group, are sustained, however, by a low burlesque metaphor of "dogginess."

Waugh employs the same mingling of the extravagant and the ironic in the structure of the novels. In the works before *Brideshead,* plot is usually farcical, a distortion of reality. Scene, or episode, on the other hand, is treated ironically through "counterpoint" or montage; the technique is most obvious in the earliest novels, and it has persisted, though significantly modified in *Brideshead* and the novels following it, right down to the Crouchback trilogy, where it is again a prominent element.

Nigel Dennis has described this technique as "high narrative flash-point"; an accomplished satirical novelist himself, Dennis admires the "sleight of hand" by which Waugh manages it.[6] His admiration is justified, for Waugh has mastered all the ironic possibilities of this technique. To begin with, "counterpointing" enables him to move about in space while remaining fixed in time and thus to spatialize his fiction, suggesting all the qualities of an atmosphere surrounding a particular group. The opening section of *Vile Bodies,* in which the Bright Young People and a number of their elders cross the English Channel from the Continent, is a good example of this use; there Waugh employs counterpoint as a means of revealing the incoherence and absurdity of life in the twenties. It also reveals the values which make such incoherence seem ridiculous. A vignette of Kitty Blackwater and Fanny Throbbing, too weak even to discuss the young men on board and in the throes of seasickness, is followed by this detail: "To Father Rothschild no passage was worse than any other. He thought of the suffering of the saints, the mutability of human nature, the Four Last Things, and between whiles repeated snatches of the penitential psalms." Immediately the scene shifts to the stateroom where Lord Outrage, the Leader of His Majesty's Opposition, is sunk in opium dreams. From a distance Mrs. Ape is heard leading a few broken voices in her famous hymn, "There Ain't No Flies on the Lamb of God."

Such counterpointing can also, through incisive contrast, develop the theme of the novel. In *Black Mischief* the essential hostility of Seth's people to civilization and the futility of his attempts to modernize are both suggested when Waugh shifts from a tea at the British legation to this scene, given in a sentence: "Sixty miles southward in the Ukaka Pass bloody bands of Sakuyu warriors played hide and seek among the rocks, chivvying the last fugitives of the army of Seyid, while behind them down the gorge, from cave villages of incalculable antiquity, the women crept out to rob the dead." When this method of spatial counterpoint is pursued at greater length in the structure of a novel, it develops dramatic irony, as in *Officers and Gentlemen.* The catastrophe on

Crete, the virtual destruction of the Halberdier units, the flagrant cowardice on every hand, and the total disillusionment of Guy Crouchback are paralleled by episodes in which Trimmer conducts a phony raid on occupied France and is then built up as a war hero to spur on the masses in the factories, who crave heroes from the lower classes.

At other times this "flash-point" technique is not spatial but essentially chronological. Abrupt and kaleidoscopic shifting from one key moment to another can also create dramatic irony. On the morning of his wedding, Paul Pennyfeather raises his liqueur glass, offering a toast to "Fortune . . . a much-maligned lady." A moment later, after a break in the text, we read, "Which of you gentlemen is Mr. Paul Pennyfeather?" The speaker is from Scotland Yard and has come to arrest Paul on a white-slavery charge. In *A Handful of Dust* Waugh uses this method with telling irony, to suggest the conflict of personalities and values which precipitates the catastrophe. For example, Tony Last returns to Hetton at dusk, admiring what he sees: "A thin mist lay breast high over the park; the turrets and battlements of the abbey stood grey and flat; the boiler man was hauling down the flag on the main tower." A moment later, after a break in the prose, Tony steps into one of the rooms he loves so well with Brenda and Mrs. Beaver, the decorator, who exclaims: "My poor Brenda, it's an appalling room."

These different but related satirical modes (irony of manner in the treatment of the *ingénus,* understatement in the characterization of some subordinate figures, varieties of burlesque in the delineation of grotesque characters) and the different but complementary structural devices (extravagance of action, irony of episode) are thus at the basis of Waugh's satirical expression. It would not be accurate to say that the modes conflict with one another. On the contrary, they operate harmoniously because Waugh has such control of the "high narrative flash-point," or the counterpoint, that he fuses the elements into a dominating detached irony. Waugh's mastery of this particular technique, the kind of skill he praised in Firbank, permits Nigel Dennis to describe him, "five characters in each hand" developing "in smoothly interlocking conversations and exits and entries, the reader's understanding of his people, their immediate situation, and the theme of the novel."[7]

CHAPTER VII

Satire and Negation

THE charges—snobbery, cruelty, and adolescence of conception—made against Waugh by a number of critics may contain some element of truth, but they do not really help us to understand the essential nature and the development of his satirical perspective. In *The Rebel* Albert Camus set forth a view of the modern intellectual as rebel; the rebel he defined as a man who rejects his condition, in society or in the cosmos, because he has a vision of a value superior to his condition. The rebel simultaneously says "no" to the world he spurns and "yes" to the world he desires. His rebellion is not merely negative, because "he is acting in the name of certain values which . . . he feels are common to himself and all men." As Camus conceived him, the rebel "implicitly brings into play a standard of values."

Strange as it may seem to associate Evelyn Waugh with the term "rebel," even as it is defined by Camus, this concept points to certain central characteristics of the satirist, and of satire. What else is the satirist but a man who rejects the behavior of those who surround him, the standards of his society, or the customs of his time, in favor of values which he regards as superior to those he disdains? The following passage from Camus seems particularly apropos to Waugh, who, in response to the disorders and confusions of his time, has turned to the oldest of the churches and to a political position so far to the right that some people, even Gilbert Pinfold's sound Tory neighbors, might regard it as "being almost as sinister as socialism."

> Rebellion is born of the spectacle of irrationality, confronted with an unjust and incomprehensible condition. But its blind impulse is to demand order in the midst of chaos, and unity in the very heart of the ephemeral. It protests, it demands, it insists that the outrage be brought to an end, and that what has up to now been built upon shifting sands should henceforth be founded on rock. Its preoccupation is to transform.[1]

Certainly the world which Evelyn Waugh represents in his early novels is irrational and incomprehensible; he has criticized that world from the position of one who insists upon order; he has found his rock, in his personal life, in the Roman Catholic church and in an extremely conservative political position. But the question remains: Has Waugh in his novels not only rejected the world which displeases him, but also simultaneously affirmed a meaningful vision of a way of life superior to that he rejects?

The satirist drawing on the aesthetic, moral, or metaphysical resources that supply his strength may make one of a number of choices. He may choose not to embody his beliefs, his notions of the good life, in his satire at all. He may insist upon so forcing those alternatives upon us that he becomes didactic. Or he may walk the sword's edge between rejection and affirmation, and give tangible expression to what he values as well as to what he scorns. Juvenal may excoriate the vileness of Rome, but he lets us hear why the good old days were good; Rabelais lambastes monastic asceticism, but he celebrates the Abbey of Thélême; Swift scorns the vices of Lilliput, but he sees some virtues there. Moreover, great satire offers as an alternative to vice and folly a value to which not only the satirist but (ideally) all men should respond. In the terms of Camus, it is a fulfilled rebellion.

When we turn to modern satirists, we note that such writers as Wyndham Lewis and Aldous Huxley have had private values to express; but only Huxley has succeeded in giving *some* degree of universality to his private views. The same two satirists, who both attempt to express their positive attitudes in explicit form, have had difficulty, however, walking that sword's edge; they are vexed by the demon of didacticism. Waugh, on the other hand, works obliquely. In addition, throughout the first stage of his career, he offers only the most fleeting glimpses into a positive and affirmative standard—Anchorage House in *Vile Bodies* and Boot Magna Hall in *Scoop*. Not until *Brideshead Revisited,* in which his Catholicism is revealed for the first time, does a positive force significantly emerge to oppose everything that the novelist rejects. Extraordinarily enough, the most striking characteristic of the early novels, the aspect which has disturbed so many of his readers and which they have perhaps attributed to childishness or snobbery or cruelty, is the absence of any positive good, either rendered or implied. In effect, then, as products of a rebellion (which in Waugh's personal life may have been fulfilled), the early novels remain generally negative and destructive; and, consequently, Waugh is criticized for lacking a high moral purpose and writing satire without a moral center.[2]

Decline and Fall, which reveals a world without consequence, suggests that its author views life very nearly in the manner of the "absurdist," the man in the first and purely nihilist stage of rebellion. (Though this attitude, I must stress, is *in no sense* formalized or intellectualized.) Albert Camus, in criticizing the sterility of the "tough" American novel of the thirties and forties, has called our attention to the function of the "innocent" or "simpleton" figure in these futile protests.[3] Although Evelyn Waugh's Paul Pennyfeather has little in common with the simpleton of the American naturalistic novel, the fact remains that he, as innocent, also plays a significant role in the pervasive negativism of the novel. As the only represented "good" in *Decline and Fall,* Paul is so passive that he is incapable not only of deliberate action but also of distinction between the apparent and the real, and so blank that he can be acted upon by vice and become a part of folly. Paul learns nothing from his experiences; he remains the same neutral being, possessing only his innocence.

The principal objects of the satire in this novel are diverse, indeed, related to one another largely by the picaresque convention: Oxford, public schools, the smart set, the white-slave trade, modern architecture, prison reformers—these are all ridiculed. Toward the close of the novel Waugh seems to be on firm conservative ground as he aims his shafts at abstractionism in the arts and, even more pointedly, at the penal reformer, Sir Wilfred Lucas-Dockery. Whereas Sir Wilfred is advised by his predecessor, a retired colonel, that "If you make prison bad enough, people'll take jolly good care to keep out of it," Sir Wilfred, the appointee of a Labour minister and the former holder of a sociology chair at a midland university, is all in favor of psychology and personal contact. He wants his prisoners to "take pride" in their prison; but the shocked reaction of one prisoner to his reforms proves that even the criminal recognizes excess: "I've been in six prisons, and I never seen nothing to touch it. Most irregular. You doesn't know where you are these days." Living in the fantasy world of his reforms, Sir Wilfred is too busy to attend to the fact that one of his kitchen workers suffers from an infectious disease of the hands; dedicated to the principle of craft training, he places sharp instruments in the hands of his prisoners, thus precipitating two attempted suicides and the horrifying murder of Prendergast.

On the other hand, nearly two thirds of the novel is devoted to a satire of "the Establishment." As the novel opens, Sniggs and Postlethwaite, two junior dons, gleefully anticipate the fines that will come to their college in consequence of the outrages to which the Bollinger Club meeting will surely lead; and Pennyfeather is sent down when the Master points out that he, unlike the Bollinger members, could not possibly pay a fine. Llanabba Castle, which aspires to all the conventions of the English preparatory school, is the quintessence of sham, and the vaunted playing fields of English schoolboy sports are a total fraud. The social structure, revealed in its major distinctions at the school sports, is treated with the greatest irreverence. Lady Circumference, one of the landed gentry, grimly enunciates "Dig it and dung it" as her guiding principle. She is just as vulgar as the bourgeois Clutterbucks, whose fortune comes from a brewery. Mrs. Beste-Chetwynde, an ornament to the fashionable city aristocracy, conducts herself like a demimondaine; she arrives at the games with her current lover, the Negro musician Chokey.

Yet in the characterization of Margot we encounter Waugh's curious ambivalence of attitude, which also persists in the novels written after his conversion to Catholicism. This lady can scarcely be regarded as anything less than depraved; the rumor that she poisoned her first husband does not fit ill with her ruthlessness as she conducts her "business" affairs and involves Pennyfeather in them. Associating her with a fortune based upon organized prostitution in South America, Waugh seems to imply that his society is now so degraded that a name "honoured in his country's history" is sustained by vice. On the other hand, Waugh is plainly enchanted by Margot; she appears in the novel, emerging from her limousine, "like the first breath of spring in the Champs Élysées." She is a creature above and beyond any moral code; and Pennyfeather accepts his imprisonment, knowing that it is inconceivable even to imagine Margot being brought to trial and imprisoned.

As the novel ends, Waugh attempts to provide some thematic justification for this curious moral confusion. Throughout the novel the satirist has worked with a distinction between the passive and the active nature; in Otto Silenus' lecture to Paul, the distinction is formulated in terms of a metaphor of the big wheel at Luna Park. This wheel symbolizes life; at the center one sees statis, at the outer rim, movement and excitement. Margot enjoys clinging to the outermost rim and holding on for dear life; Silenus has nearly achieved the still point at the center of the turning world. Pennyfeather had climbed, or rather been dragged, onto the wheel for a brief moment, but he belongs in the bleachers watching the spinning wheel. He is static, Margot, "dynamic"; and the two are "quite different species spiritually."

Pennyfeather accepts this explanation, and, later, when he encounters Peter Pastmaster at Oxford, he agrees with Peter's assertion that "We're different somehow." This formulation of the attitude permeating the novel might appear to be nothing more than a distinction between those who act and those who sit and watch; but the implications of the argument are much more extreme. The satirist seems to imply that amoralism may be justified by the very nature of things, that there are those such as Paul, who live within the law and are judged by it, while there are others, such as Peter and his mother, who, by virtue of their dynamism and, perhaps, their position, are outside the "whole code of ready-made honour," inherited by Paul but "inapplicable" to them.

In his recent Writers and Critics pamphlet on Waugh, Malcolm Bradbury raises this issue of moral consistency. He argues (with respect to *Black Mischief*) that Waugh depends for "consistency" on a "dominant comic tone"; but then he goes on to assert that "Waugh's comic approach . . . absolves him from conventional construction, enabling a wild fictional world and creating for those critics who seek to find a consistent vein of value or purpose in such books a difficult problem."[4] Bradbury's defense is subtle, but not entirely persuasive, since it involves a rapid shifting of critical terms—from "tone" to "structure." Too many readers who neither insist that every novel be a "moral fable," nor demand that a satirist have a one-track mind, are conscious, at times, of inconsistencies in Waugh's perspective, or tone. And satire which does not spring from a certain consistency of value and attitude leads only to moral confusion. In *Decline and Fall,* to consider the case in point, after brilliantly exposing the social foolishness which is causing the fall of a great empire, Evelyn Waugh radically alters his point of view and the values implicit in it. Alas, it is as if he had suddenly pulled the rug out from under his own feet.

Vile Bodies, written during the year of his conversion, reveals no such uncertainty or moral ambivalence, and Waugh does not wait until the end to articulate his theme, which is expressed with assurance throughout. While the picaresque convention, much transformed, provides the skeleton of the structure, Waugh has aimed his satire far more precisely than he did in *Decline and Fall*; and the activities of the Bright Young People introduce us to the futility and rootlessness of life in the twenties. The novel is written, as was its predecessor, out of a conviction that the modern world is absurd, and the speech of Chastity in the last pages embodies that attitude. Recruited by Margot Beste-Chetwynde for her "entertainment" enterprises in Buenos Aires, the former angel with Mrs. Ape was called back to England when war came. Then Chastity "was with" the troops on Salisbury Plain:

That was swell. They called me Bunny—I don't know why. Then they sent me over here and I was with the Canadians, what they called me wasn't nice, and then they left me behind when they retreated and I took up with some foreigners. They were nice too, though they *were* fighting against the English. Then *they* ran away, and the lorry I was in got stuck in the ditch, so I got in with some other foreigners who were on the same side as the English, and they were beasts, but I met an American doctor who had white hair and he called me Emily because he said I reminded him of his daughter back home, so he took me to Paris and we had a lovely week till he took up with another girl in a night club, so he left me behind in Paris when he went back to the front, and I hadn't no money and they made a fuss about my passport, so they called me *numero mille soixante dix-huit*, and they sent me and a lot of other girls off to the East to be with the soldiers there. At least they would have done only the ship got blown up, so I was rescued and the French sent me up here in a train with some different girls who were very unrefined. Then I was in a tin hut with the girls, and then yesterday they had friends and I was alone, so I went for a walk, and when I came back the hut was gone and the girls were gone, and there didn't seem anyone anywhere until you came in your car, and now I don't rightly know where I am. *My*, isn't war awful?

Lust, violence, loyalty, nationality, identity, sentiment, life, and death—all are equally casual and fortuitous; and Chastity, incapable as she is of moral distinctions, is the appropriate medium to express the incoherence.

Once again, Waugh depicts innocence in his hero, and in his heroine also. The situation of Adam and Nina, however, is more pathetic than that of Pennyfeather, because they are conscious of what is happening to them. In a feverish nightmare, Miss Runcible (who ran into a civic monument when she lost control of her racing auto and is to die of her injuries) imagines that she and all her friends are driving round and round in a race, unable to stop, surrounded by an audience of gossip writers and social climbers "all shouting at us at once to go faster, and car after car . . . crashing." Her nightmare, reminiscent of the futile taxi ride of Gumbril and Myra Viveash in Huxley's *Antic Hay*, symbolizes the life from which Adam and Nina, in rare moments of tranquillity, withdraw in loathing and disgust. Adam reflects upon the feverish round of parties which are analogous to Miss Runcible's motor race:

. . . Masked parties, Savage parties, Victorian parties, Greek parties, Wild West parties, Russian parties, Circus parties, parties where one had to dress as someone else, almost naked parties in St. John's Wood . . . dull dances in London and comic dances in Scotland and disgusting dances in Paris—all that succession and repetition of massed humanity. . . . Those vile bodies. . . .

So he leans his forehead to cool it on Nina's arm, and she murmurs "I *know,* darling."

Adam and Nina are pitiful because they do somehow know that something is wrong. During one episode, Ginger takes Nina on a flight in his airplane; he looks down at the earth beneath them and tries to remember some lines from a "blue poetry book" describing "This scepter'd isle, this earth of majesty, this something or other Eden." Nina also looks and—seeing arterial roads, factories, a disused canal, bungalows, and overhead wire cables—decides that she is going to be sick. In addition, they are pathetic because they do not, as Pennyfeather does, retain their quality of innocence; they become a part of what nauseates them. Adam "sells" Nina to Ginger Littlejohn to pay a debt, and she marries Ginger.

In a prefatory author's note, Waugh explains the chronology of the novel, concluding with the mordant sarcasm, "Christmas is observed by the Western Church on December 25th." During these observances, which can be mentioned with such historic detachment, Nina and Adam visit Doubting All; there they witness a filmed life of Wesley, an "All-Talkie super-religious film" involving a duel between Wesley and Whitfield over Selina, Countess of Huntingdom; they observe the intermittent warfare between Mr. Blount and the Rector, they share punch with the carolers and toasts with the servants, and attend matins—rituals that seem to be merely outmoded and dim reminders of an occasion which must at some time in the past have meant something. As the day closes, they hear that war has been declared. During that war (against an unnamed enemy and for unspecified reasons), Adam learns that Nina is to bear his child.

Only Father Rothschild, the plotting Jesuit, is able to make sense out of these antics and to explain both the war and the Bright Young People: the war is the inevitable consequence of "a radical instability in our whole world order" (which explains why the adversary in, and motivation of, the war do not matter). The Bright Young People are a reflection of that disorder. But, Rothschild explains, the younger generation is not willing, as their elders are, to "muddle along" making the best of a bad job. They do not say, with his church, "If a thing's worth doing at all, it's worth doing well," but instead, having "got hold of another end of the stick," they say, "If a thing's not worth doing well, it's not worth doing at all." But Father Rothschild, for all his knowingness, returns us to the nihilism of *Decline and Fall.* Although he can explain, he offers no alternative; the plotting in which he engages for the Prufrockian Lord Outrage is the most futile kind of muddling through. While Adam would give anything for something "different" and is convinced that "everything" has gone wrong, he does not know how to achieve the "different." He has "nothing," the word Miss Runcible hears over and over again as she enters her last coma and the frantic race ends for her.

Evelyn Waugh has been called the first writer to explore shamelessness.[5] The hero of *Black Mischief,* his third satire, is Basil Seal, whose shamelessness obliterates that of Margot Beste-Chetwynde. Recounting Seal's adventures in an African kingdom, the novel burlesques the ambition of Seth, the youthful emperor, to "modernize" and civilize his kingdom. However, Waugh does not proceed on the assumption that the "civilization" Seth vainly hopes to import is superior to the barbarism of Azania. In common with its predecessors, *Black Mischief* is essentially destructive and negative. Basil Seal is another member of a generation which believes that "if a thing's not worth doing well, it's not worth doing at all." In England he finds nothing worthy of his attention, preferring to seek out situations where he can manipulate power. Lady Seal engages in a "nursery game of 'let's pretend' " with her adviser, an "old booby," Sir Joseph Mannering, as they plan to convert Basil, who has disgraced himself as a candidate for Parliament, into a respectable barrister. It is precisely this kind of "bogosity" that Basil Seal hopes to escape, and he retreats to Azania where he becomes Seth's "man of progress and culture," and for a while enjoys playing his own kind of nursery game as Minister of Modernisation. But Basil soon loses all confidence in the permanence of Seth's One Year Plan, which proves to be as much a sham as life in England.

In Waugh's handling of Basil Seal and his adventures, however, we find the same ambivalence of attitude which is present in *Decline and Fall.* The daughter of the British envoy in Azania, Prudence, who has been writing something she calls the *Panorama of Life* and developing source material in an affair with the legation secretary, immediately sees Basil as a source of new material for her literary endeavors. Waugh's treatment of the inevitable seduction is indirect, but an image which functions as "objective correlative" mirrors his attitude toward the incident. When Prudence visits Basil, she finds him in a room rank with tobacco smoke:

> Basil, in shirt sleeves, rose from the deck chair to greet her. He threw the butt of his Burma cheroot into the tin hip bath which stood unemptied at the side of the bed; it sizzled and went out and floated throughout the afternoon, slowly unfurling in the soapy water. He bolted the door. . . . At first neither spoke. Presently she said, "You might have shaved," and then, "Please help with my boots."
>
> Below, in the yard, Madame Youkoumian upbraided a goat. Strips of sunlight traversed the floor as an hour passed. In the bath water, the soggy stub of tobacco emanated a brown blot of juice.

The counterpoint technique is so brilliant in this passage that it provokes disgust. Even Graham Greene, a master hand with sordid details and seedy rooms, has no more sickening image than this of the cigar stump in the hip bath as a commentary on lust. Later in the relationship Basil tells Prudence, "You're a grand girl . . . and I'd like to eat you." She promises, "So you shall, my sweet . . . anything you want." And he does. At the feast which follows the cremation of the deposed Emperor Seth, the drunken headman draws Basil's attention to his elegant new headdress—the red beret Prudence had worn as she escaped from the British legation, under imagined threat of siege by the natives. When Basil demands to know the whereabouts of the white woman, the savage, patting his "distended paunch," explains, "Why here. . . . You and I and the big chiefs—we have just eaten her." Waugh has traced this relationship without comment or analysis and has not described Basil's reaction to the savage's statement, but the bearing of the details is unmistakable. The kind of "civilized" promiscuity in which Prudence and Basil indulge is actually another form of savagery, and Basil's desire is nothing more than the cannibalism of which Prudence's fate is an *outré* symbol. Basil's "civilization," in short, is barbarism.

The author's sympathy, however, is, as earlier suggested, very much with Basil Seal. Indeed, Basil has certain virtues; he is loyal to Seth to the end, and he is unmistakably courageous. It may be argued that a sympathetic attitude toward his shamelessness is another satirical pose, for Basil's outrageousness, like the innocence of Pennyfeather, casts into bold relief the folly of everyone around him. Nevertheless, if England is beyond hope, if Lady Seal and Lord Joseph Mannering are foolish, if Seth is absurd and presumptuous, if the Azanians are incorrigible and irremediable savages, by what standard is Basil to be measured? The Prudence sequence supplies one answer; the romanticizing of the boy-man who is still playing pirate and Happy Families gives another. Edmund Wilson, who praised the early novels of Waugh because he found nothing "schematic" or "doctrinaire" in them, concluded that "The savagery he is afraid of is somehow the same thing as the audacity that delights him."[6] Exactly the point. Whereas Waugh despises the Azanians for their savagery, he seems to admire the savagery of Basil Seal.

At the close of *Black Mischief,* Sonia Trumpington reluctantly admits to Alastair her fear that Basil is going to turn serious on them—the only indication of a positive value emerging from the Azanian experience. However, in *Put Out More Flags,* an account of the opening year of the Second World War, we find the same shameless Seal, older but no less adept as an exploiter of the weak. In this novel, Waugh continues a trend he had begun in *Scoop,* a satire of the newspaper world and of contemporary power politics as they influence undeveloped nations. In *Scoop,* for the first time Waugh adumbrated an alternative to the decadent civilization he despised, as he represented, by means of a framing technique, William Boot's life at Boot Magna Hall and his refusal of an attractive permanent position with the *Daily Beast* in favor of seclusion and order. In *Put Out More Flags,* national revival, the "Churchillian renaissance," emerges as the most ample rejection of the nihilism which dominated the earlier books. Peter Pastmaster appears in uniform and Sam Browne belt and, motivated by dynastic impulses, marries a young woman who recognizes an innocent beneath the exterior of a "rip." Alastair Trumpington, jealous as a schoolboy of Peter's uniform, joins the ranks of enlisted men and, inspired by schoolboy honor, refuses to accept a promotion. He is expiating for the thirties, for, as Sonia explains, "he went into the ranks as a kind of penance or whatever it's called." Finally, delighted by the prospect of knives, Tommy guns, and rope-soled shoes, Alastair volunteers for special service. His associates include Peter and, in his last-minute conversion to patriotism, Basil Seal. That "old booby" Sir Joseph enunciates the meaning of these events: "There's a new spirit abroad."

As much as anything, the new spirit is evident in Waugh's handling of his material in such a way that it no longer expresses futility. For in these two works he opposes what is ridiculed with values that have been his from the very beginning. (The emphasis, which in *Scoop* falls on the nursery as an alternative to disorder and in *Put Out More Flags* on schoolboy enthusiasms as a concomitant of patriotism, permits writers such as D. S. Savage to accuse Waugh of radical immaturity of view.) Two other observations must be made. First of all, one positive alternative to social and personal disorder offered by *Put Out More Flags* is war, indicating the topical and ephemeral quality of this affirmative element in the work; and the rollicking wartime enthusiasm which buoys up the satire did not survive beyond this novel. Secondly, neither of the novels makes an artistic advance over its predecessors, and the satires lack the resonance and the incisiveness of the other early novels. The striking fact, however, is that Waugh has begun to organize and shape his material in such a way that it will both reject and affirm. It was probably inevitable that eventually his deeper religious and social values would emerge as positive elements in his work. *Scoop* and *Put Out More Flags,* which repeat the techniques and devices that Waugh had already mastered, point toward later developments in his career.

Of the early, predominantly negative novels, *A Handful of Dust* is the masterpiece and perhaps also the finest of all Waugh's works. No uncertainty, no ambivalence of attitude mars its perspective; it is a tour de force of irony. Extravagance and absurdity of action have been restrained, and the broader satiric modes have been eschewed in favor of the ironic, which, as the most detached and uncommitted of the tones on the satiric speculum, perfectly coincides with Waugh's early disinclination to make any absolute assertion of positive value. Instead, with classical restraint, precision, and economy, Waugh reveals the baseness akin to evil which exists beneath the surface gloss of the fashionable world. The subtle instrument of evaluation which his irony has become supplies the means of portraying—without invoking a double standard—not only his hero and heroine but also his villains, the riffraff of the *haut monde,* while at the same time he leaves no doubt as to who is sympathetic and who despicable.

After deserting her husband, Tony, accepting with relief the news of her son's death (she feared that it was her lover who had died), and suggesting that Tony sell his inherited home to support a new marriage for her, Brenda Last wonders if Tony's expedition to Brazil is safe. Jock de Menzies responds: "The whole world is civilized now isn't it?" Superficially, the events of the novel might be taken to mean that it is, for in the midst of the Brazilian jungle Tony Last encounters Mr. Todd, the natural son of a Christian missionary, who is unable to read but just loves to listen to Dickens. On the other hand, in *A Handful of Dust,* where everything is inverted, it is necessary to turn the side of each coin. The terrible irony of Mr. Todd's imprisonment of Tony is that nothing the half-savage does is any worse than what has been done by the near-savages in England. The answer the novel gives to Jock's question is: "No, the whole civilized world is turning primitive." Even the chapter headings provide an ironic reinforcement of this theme. The opening one, "Du Côté de Chez Beaver," reveals the sham respectability of Mrs. Beaver and John; it is paralleled by the penultimate "Du Côté de Chez Todd," which reveals the sham civilization of the converted native.

Just as Wyndham Lewis in *The Revenge for Love* saw sham at the "false bottom" of the intellectual bohemia of the thirties, so Waugh recognizes it as the basis of the sophisticated London set of the period. Mrs. Beaver entertains an ill-assorted party, all gossip column "names," at a fashionable restaurant; but she is paid to do so. Beaver's club has an "elegant Georgian facade and finely panelled rooms," but its antiquity is "spurious" and the club is of recent origin. This hollow and inadequate young man hovers over his telephone awaiting last-minute invitations from disappointed hostesses; and he never refuses an invitation, even knowing that he has been asked only because he is the last man available.

The ladies with whom Brenda associates are equally bogus. Polly Cockpurse, on her ascent of the social ladder, has married an insignificant nobleman; working slowly but assiduously she has achieved a position of social eminence which compels guests to call her before arriving with strangers. Her friends purchase her used gowns. Princess Jenny Abdul Akbar gains access to this set by announcing herself an escapee from a Moulay's harem. When Jock de Menzies arrives at Brenda's flat to announce the death of the Lasts' son, John Andrew, Jenny is there to exclaim, with artificial horror, *"Little Jimmy."* Brenda enters this world of sham when, bored after seven years of life at Hetton, she takes as her lover the first available young man and begins the deception of Tony. At this she is remarkably successful. While Polly's set applauds, Tony, who "had got into the habit of loving and trusting Brenda," remains innocent. Finally deserted by Brenda, he finds himself "in a world suddenly bereft of order," wherein all accepted values are dislocated. To establish evidence for a divorce to which he has agreed, Tony goes to a seaside hotel with a young woman who incongruously insists on bringing her daughter. The detective employed by his solicitors is shocked: "Most irregular. Sets a nasty respectable note bringing a kid into it." Later, when Brenda's demands become exorbitant and Tony refuses to go through with the divorce, most people accept Brenda's view that he has behaved in a "monstrous" way.

In view of the treatment he receives at the hands of the "savages at home" and the savage in Brazil, Tony Last, "the civilized" man in a "helpless plight,"[7] might easily have been sentimentalized. Waugh is too aware of his antihero's inadequacies for this to happen; innocence, attractive in a number of earlier characters, is here the subject of a searching irony. Tony Last is decent, honest, trusting, affectionate, boyish; he is devoted to his home and everything it signifies in the way of tradition, custom, and ceremony; and he is a regular churchgoer. All this is not enough; ritual observance, an undemanding Anglicanism, boyish innocence, and devotion to the gothic past may be admirable by contrast to Mrs. Beaver's flats and Polly Cockpurse's secondhand dresses, but they fail Tony when he is tested. At the time of John Andrew's accidental death, Tony sends the rector away, admitting that the last thing he wants to talk about at such a time is religion. So he turns instead, as an escape from thought, to a "child's game," the only card game he knows, with Mrs. Rattery:

> They each took a pack and began dealing. Soon a pair of eights appeared. "Bow-wow," said Mrs. Rattery scooping in the cards.
>
> Another pair. "Bow-wow," said Mrs. Rattery. "You know you aren't putting your heart into this."
>
> "Oh," said Tony. "Coop-coop-coop."
>
> Presently he said again, "Coop-coop-coop."
>
> "Don't be dumb," said Mrs. Rattery, "that isn't a pair. . . ."
>
> They were still playing when Albert came in to draw the curtains. . . . They stopped . . . when they found that Albert was in the room.
>
> "What must that man have thought?" said Tony, when he had gone out.
>
> ("Sitting there clucking like a 'en," Albert reported, "and the little fellow lying dead upstairs.")

Albert has a point.

Just as ironic is the treatment of Tony's search for "a City." When his gothic world comes to grief, with Brenda's departure, when the glittering armor, the "embroidered feet," "the cream and dappled unicorns" have "fled," he foolishly flees his unhappiness, accompanying Dr. Messenger in search of a fabled city in the jungle, which begins, in his imagination, to take on the gothic appearance of Hetton. But if Mrs. Beaver's flats are not comparable to Hetton's gothic, neither is Tony's Gothic City comparable to the City of God, a search for which, Waugh hints, might have saved him. When at last the "gates . . . open before him and trumpets" sound "saluting his arrival," when he sights the "gilded cupolas and spires of alabaster," the trumpets and cupolas are the hallucinations of malaria which mock his entry into the village of Mr. Todd. And in another delirium resulting from his fever, Tony is finally forced to recognize that he has been living on an illusion, that a retreat into the gothic past is impossible: "There is no City. Mrs. Beaver has covered it with chromium plating and converted it into flats. Three guineas a week with a separate bathroom. Very suitable for base love. And Polly will be there. She and Mrs. Beaver under the fallen battlements."

Tony Last is perhaps the most sympathetic character in Evelyn Waugh's entire canon. He demands our sympathy because he alone among the hollow men and women of the novel is devoted to some kind of purpose and some kind of order, but even more because, however attractive his allegiances are, in a chromium-plated world they are not strong enough to permit his survival.

Two perceptive writers, Edmund Wilson and Stephen Spender, have described, in somewhat different terms, the quality which they find in this work. Wilson speaks of the pervasive sense of terror "which is the whole motivation of the book but of which the characters are not shown to be conscious and upon which one cannot put one's finger in any specific passage."[8] Spender notes "incipient tragedy" and argues that "within a situation where people act ruthlessly and selfishly, tragedy, as it were, may be distributed over their lives, though each may be incapable of feeling its intensity."[9] That both critics should have similar reactions to the novel, though one speaks in terms of "terror" and the other in terms of "tragedy," can perhaps be traced to the quality of the irony, which produces not laughter but pain.

Little has been written about the relation between the irony of satire and the irony of tragedy, perhaps because there are variable and shifting borderlands which cannot easily be plotted. David Worcester, in his book on satire, seems to assume that the irony of tragedy is satirical, and he points out that "If irony injects an element of comedy into tragedy, no less does it inject tragic feeling into comedy."[10] Another writer questions Worcester's assumption and argues that "dramatic irony occurs often without any satirical implications," but he does not go on to explore the question.[11]

It would seem to be the case that the irony of the Greek dramatists or of Ibsen is altogether different in quality from the irony which is one of the principal elements of satire. That marked distinction is due in part to the fact that the irony of tragedy involves fatal and terrifying consequences, but also to the fact that the impulse to criticize or ridicule, always present in satire, is not a dominant element of the tragic spirit. The pervasive sense of tragicality or of terror which the reader feels in *A Handful of Dust* may perhaps be attributed to the approximation of its irony to the irony of tragedy. In themselves the characters do not approach the tragic. Nor is the novel, of course, a tragedy. *A Handful of Dust* moves somehow in the direction of the tragic as the satirical impulse to criticize and ridicule shades into that irony ordinarily associated with nonsatiric expression. Standing in the midst of the shifting borderlands between two modes of expression, it is, nevertheless, perhaps the best product of the whole satirical tendency in the modern novel. Waugh has created a masterpiece of its kind, a brilliant example of the satirical "no," unaccompanied by any positive affirmation.

Part Four

AFFIRMATION AND APOLOGY

CHAPTER VIII

The Phenomenon of Conversion

George Bernard Shaw once observed that "those who give up Materialism whilst clinging to Rationalism generally either relapse into abject submission to the most paternal of the Churches, or are caught by the attempts, constantly renewed, of mystics to found a new faith by rationalising on the hollowness of materialism."[1] Though Shaw unfortunately obscured his meaning by using the term "rationalism" not "as classified in books, but as apparent in men" and by lumping together as "rationalists" all those who did not accept his own vitalist faith,[2] he did point to a certain dichotomy in the tendency to conversion among modern English men of letters, a tendency which has had a pronounced effect on the literature of this century.

Escaping from materialism, rationalism, utilitarianism, Darwinism, secularism, humanism, liberalism, science, or progress, English men of letters have been entering the paternalistic churches or, with some help from the mystics, inventing religions of their own. Shaw, like his master Samuel Butler, followed the latter course, as did William Butler Yeats, D. H. Lawrence, and Aldous Huxley. T. S. Eliot and W. H. Auden are the most notable converts to Anglicanism, while from the nineties to the present a steady procession of literary converts has taken the path to Rome.

These conversions are another manifestation of the romantic artist's rebellion against the condition of man in the modern world. It is possible to regard Blake and Coleridge—the one inventing a metaphysical system, the other adopting religious orthodoxy—as the prototypes of all these converts. To be sure, the dreadful hypostatized condition against which romantic artists from Blake to Waugh have rebelled has differed slightly from time to time and from man to man—from the early Romantics' "rationalism" to Waugh's "Modern Age in arms," for example. All the romantic rebels, whether "heretics" or converts, have been protesting against the spiritual aridity which they have sensed in modern civilization. That they have often been confused in their revolts, have often mistaken the real enemy, and have often ascribed to their opponents motives and attitudes which those opponents have lacked, is perhaps less important than that they have frequently believed the modern world to be materialist, sterile, and futile.

While conformity to the dogmas of the Church has lent the rebellions of Roman Catholic literary men a kind of consistency which is absent in the protests and commitments of the heterodox and unorthodox, ample evidence indicates that the tendency to Roman Catholicism is not distinct from the larger movement. For example, while at school Lionel Johnson was interested in a possible synthesis of "Christ, Buddha, Swedenborg, Kant, Fichte, Jacobi, Emerson, *et hoc genus omne*," and he was reading Sinnett's *Esoteric Buddhism*; later he turned to the Church.[3] Even G. K. Chesterton, that pillar of orthodoxy, was early attracted to Theosophy.[4] An essential distinction probably does exist, however, between those men who have chosen Roman Catholicism or Anglicanism and those who have formulated private systems: between those, such as Eliot and Waugh, who require the certitude of a traditional and logically formulated body of doctrine, and those, such as Yeats or Huxley, for whom skepticism has precluded the possibility of adherence to one of the traditional churches, but whose emotion, spirit, and imagination have at the same time demanded a substitute religion.

Evelyn Waugh and his contemporary Graham Greene have little in common with the generation of aggressive Roman Catholic writers which preceded them, that of those hearty and heady optimists Chesterton and Belloc; but they do have much in common with the Anglo Catholic T. S. Eliot. (For example, Waugh has observed that Chesterton was a "sweet and virtuous man" but "the poetic and romantic child of a smug tradition."[5]) As we have seen, Waugh's early, predominantly negative satires reflect the spirit of futility and despair which pervades Eliot's *The Waste Land* and focus on many of the same deficiencies of the modern world—its rootlessness, its abandoned materialism, its sterility, its chaos, its valuelessness. Just as in his prose Eliot has blamed the nastiness of the present on "liberalism" and "Science,"[6] so Greene and Waugh have found appropriate abstractions to describe the cause of all they abhor in modern society. Greene writes of "the peril of extinction" to which "centuries of cerebration have brought us";[7] and Waugh, explaining his conversion, denounces "Scepticism" and "the materialistic, mechanized state."[8]

We must, however, probably turn to what these writers have envisioned in their works as partaking of evil or disorder to understand why they withdrew in disgust from their society and sought refuge in their churches. The shadow cast by Sweeney straddled in the sun, the murderous paws of Rachel née Rabinovitch, the typist and the young man carbuncular, the ruined cities, and the hooded hordes; the world of gangsters, spies, and secret agents, the hundreds of seedy rooms, the furtive lusts, the lavatory flushing at the moment of betrayal; the frenzied drive of Miss Runcible, the dead girl's beret on the cannibal's head, the sermon of Mrs. Melrose-Ape, the slap-up flats to fill a long-felt need, the set of Dickens in the jungle—these symbols, images, and details, which embody the visions of Eliot, Greene, and Waugh, explain better than the abstract, pejorative epithets of controversy what characteristics of the century led to their conversion. The vulgarity, tawdriness, and corruption of an urban and industrialized society, all heightened by the social disorders consequent upon vast international conflicts, are the facts of experience to which these men of sensibility would not submit.

Karl Adam, considering the revival of the Catholic church in the years following the First World War, wrote: "We have witnessed the collapse of great states and traditions of culture. On the battlefields of the Great War lie strewn the ruins of former political and economic greatness." And so, he said, "amid the desolation of the present" the eye is inevitably drawn "to that world embracing society which in the midst of this ruin stands like some unshaken rocky peak."[9] Reflecting the same distaste for the desolation of the present, a decade later Graham Greene wrote of his religion: "Even if it were all untrue and there was no God, surely life was happier with the enormous supernatural promise than with the petty social fulfilment, the tiny pension and the machine-made furniture." Without the promise, he would feel, there is nothing: "Just the drugstore and the Coca-Cola, the hamburger, the graceless, sinless empty chromium world."[10] And Waugh, explaining his conversion, has written: "Those who have read my works will perhaps understand the character of the world into which I exuberantly launched myself. Ten years of that world sufficed to show me that life there, or anywhere, was unintelligible and unendurable without God."[11] Waugh was forced, as were Greene and Eliot, by the extremity of his revulsion from the dominant tendencies of his time to accept some value which would transcend the immediate, just as in his satire he was forced to express some affirmative value in the midst of his negative criticism. He resembles the type of modern convert described by Karl Adam—"sated with negation," he desired "to affirm."

In the Roman Catholic church Waugh found a tradition which could sustain him, a principle of order which he could assert against the disintegrating forces surrounding him, and a logically formulated body of dogma which could satisfy his need for a rational foundation for his belief. If these are not the only elements of his faith, they are its essential public characteristics, and they are the religious values implicit in his later satires.

Waugh was conscious that in England the Anglican church had all the aesthetic appeal which the Roman Catholic church possessed on the Continent, and he seems to have regretted that the great cathedrals, the ceremonies surrounding the throne, the social organization of the country parishes, the culture of Oxford and Cambridge, the liturgy composed "in the heyday of English prose style," were all the property of the Church of England. He was also apparently distressed that, in England, Catholics must "meet in modern buildings, often of deplorable design, and are usually served by simple Irish missionaries." Indeed, the priests in his novels are not particularly attractive types, and they are sharply satirized. Father Mackay in *Brideshead* is a "genial" and "simple" Glasgow-Irishman, but even the saintly Cordelia considers him fair target for her jokes; in *Men at Arms* another Irish priest, a recent graduate of Maynooth who appears briefly, seems to be rooting for Hitler against the English. He is a *most* unpleasant sort.

Despite the rawness of church architecture and of Irish missionaries, Waugh has stated that the permanence of the Roman Catholic tradition, in England as well as on the Continent, is inescapable. "The Catholic structure still lies lightly buried beneath every phase of English life; history, topography, law, archeology everywhere reveal Catholic origins." This devotion to a continuous and unbroken tradition does establish one point of contact at least between Waugh and that "poetic and romantic child of a smug tradition," G. K. Chesterton. Waugh's observation that the "heresies and schisms" of Christian history have always been "local" and "temporary," serving only to reveal the "universal, eternal character of the church,"[12] reminds us that Chesterton offered as one explanation of his conversion the fact that "while heretical creeds have risen up to destroy each other, the Church has clung to its unchanging doctrines."[13]

One of Waugh's briefer satires, a doctrinaire little work called "Out of Depth," embodies this traditionalist attitude, this conviction that the church alone is eternal and unchanging amidst the disorders of history. Rip Van Winkle, an American Catholic, and Alastair Trumpington, leaving one of Margot Metroland's dinners somewhat befuddled by wine, fall into the company of a black magician, who sends Alastair back into the time of Ethelred the Unready, and Rip forward into the twenty-fifth century. Rip discovers that the jungle has crept back into the heart of London, that mud flats submerge the Strand, and that Englishmen of the period, living in wattled huts, have reverted to the condition of savages. Yet the Church survives. The Negroes who visit the village of London on a trading mission are now the colonizers. Sold into slavery by the natives of London, Rip is taken to the coast, where he sees barracks, a government house, a mission, and a black man in the robes of a Dominican. Finally he attends a Mass:

> Rip knew that out of strangeness, there had come into being something familiar; a shape in chaos. Something was being done that Rip knew; something that twenty-five centuries had not altered; of his own childhood which survived the age of the world. In a log-built church at the coast town he was squatting among a native congregation. . . . The priest turned toward them his bland, black face.
>
> 'Ite, missa est.'

Regaining consciousness in a hospital, Rip immediately calls for a priest; he then learns that even the profane Alastair, raving about a dream of the Middle Ages, has also sent for a priest.

Rip's experience as he witnesses the Mass reveals another of Catholicism's appeals for Evelyn Waugh. The ritual performed by the black priest is "a shape in chaos"; the traditional and eternal form of the rite brings order into a world of disorder, into the violent past and the barbaric future. Waugh, in common with many other modern men, seems to be haunted by a nightmarish vision of the turbulence not only of his own time but of the past and future as well, and the intensity of his dread of chaos is equaled only by his devotion to the principles of control and stability. "The Incarnation," he asserts, reflecting upon the aeons before Christ's birth, "restored order." Man at last had been given an "open divinely constituted human society."[14]

When Waugh speaks of civilization, he does not mean what he satirizes as "talking cinemas and tinned food . . . surgery and hygienic houses" but rather "the whole moral and artistic organization of Europe." This civilization he regards as inseparable from the conservative role of the Church. At the time of his conversion, Waugh explained that the confusion of moral and social standards to which Europe was witness and the emergence of "the materialistic, mechanized state, already existent in Russia and rapidly spreading south and west," were consequences of the loss of faith in Christianity. He concluded, therefore, that it was no longer possible, as it had been in the time of Gibbon, to accept "civilization" and reject Christianity. Civilization—its order and continuity—"came into being through Christianity, and without it has no significance or power to command allegiance"; indeed, by itself, he argues, "it has not the power of survival."[15] Without doubt, Evelyn Waugh's political and social conservatism is inextricably linked to the conservatism of his particular version of Roman Catholicism. The "ultra" quality of that religious conservatism has been most recently expressed in the preface to *Sword of Honour,* where Waugh reveals that he has been so profoundly disturbed by the recent doctrinal and liturgical reforms of Roman Catholicism —modernism's cruelest victory—that he can regard his trilogy as a kind of obituary for the religious practices and conceptions of his youth.

The Catholicism of Evelyn Waugh is rationalistic and antimystical. Waugh made the leap of faith, of course, and made it absolutely and totally.

> It was self evident to me [he has explained] that no heresy or schism could be right and the Church wrong. It was possible that all were wrong. . . . But if the Christian revelation was true, then the Church was the society founded by Christ. . . . This proposition seemed so plain to me that it admitted of no discussion.[16]

Once beyond this area of total, irrational commitment, however, Waugh's Catholicism lays great emphasis on logic, clarity, and reason. He rejected the other churches because "it seems to me a necessary sign of completeness and vitality in a religious body that its teaching shall be coherent and consistent."[17] He is distrustful of any attitude or expression which suggests irrationality or mysticism. The early satirical sections of D. H. Lawrence's *The Plumed Serpent* Waugh has termed "superb," but he found that in the rest of the book Lawrence's "neurotic imagination" created "one of the silliest stories in recent literature."[18] Even fellow Catholic Graham Greene bothers Waugh, who is disturbed by the "mystical" element in *The Heart of the Matter.*[19] And *The End of the Affair,* which suggests that the saintliness of the heroine may be ascribed to her baptism in infancy by a Catholic priest, causes Waugh to snap: "Mr. Greene knows very well that she would have been as surely baptised by the local vicar."[20]

The essence of Catholicism for Waugh is that it dissipates obscurity and ambiguity; the Church has brought mystery out into the light of reason. When, for example, he visited the monastery at Debra Lebanos, he was even more appalled by the nature of the Abyssinian Catholic ritual than he was by the filthiness and ignorance of the monks. The "unintelligible," "secret," and "confused" rites performed in a church wherein the sanctuary was hidden from the worshipers semed to Waugh to have little to do with Christianity, much to do with the obfuscation he associated with the non-Christian sects of the East. Nothing could better characterize the rationalistic quality of his faith than his own words about this experience:

> At Debra Lebanos I suddenly saw the classic basilica and open altar as a great positive achievement, a triumph of light over darkness consciously accomplished, and I saw theology as the science of simplification by which nebulous and elusive ideas are formalised and made intelligible and exact. I saw the Church of the first century as a dark and hidden thing, as dark and hidden as the seed germinating in the womb. . . . The priests hid their offices practicing trades; their identity was known only to initiates. . . . And the pure nucleus of the truth lay in the minds of the people, encumbered with superstitions, gross survivals of the paganism in which they had been brought up; hazy and obscene nonsense seeping from the other esoteric cults of the Near East, magical infections from the conquered barbarian. And I began to see how those obscure sanctuaries had grown, with the clarity of Western reason, into the great open altars of Catholic Europe, where Mass is said in a flood of light.[21]

To be sure, that prose, quivering with emotion, perhaps reconciles thought and feeling in the artist. In any case, its rationalistic substance surely indicates that Evelyn Waugh could never have taken the way of Yeats, Lawrence, and Huxley.

CHAPTER IX

Satire and Sentiment in Brideshead Revisited

BRIDESHEAD REVISITED, less a satire than a romance, marks the first accomplishment of the second stage of Evelyn Waugh's career. Though something of the old, hard brilliance remains, there is a new tone of lush nostalgia in this work, the first of Waugh's novels in which his Roman Catholicism is pervasive. Indeed, excepting *Helena,* it is Waugh's only novel to date in which a religious theme has been dominant; although Guy Crouchback is a Catholic and Roman Catholicism figures constantly in *Men at Arms, Officers and Gentlemen,* and *Unconditional Surrender,* the essential theme of these three volumes is the total collapse of civilized values which is the concomitant of war. In effect, in *Brideshead Revisited* Evelyn Waugh turned from the nihilistic rejection of his early satires to an affirmative commitment; to satisfy the other impulse of the artist-rebel, as Albert Camus has described him, Waugh affirmed a vision which he believed gave unity to life. *Brideshead Revisited* was his "attempt to trace the divine purpose in a pagan world."[1]

Reviewing *Brideshead,* Edmund Wilson, who had most highly praised the earlier satires, concluded that in this more normal world the novelist "no longer knows his way"; he found the novel to be "disastrous."[2] By contrast, a reviewer for the *Catholic World* judged *Brideshead* "a work of art."[3]

These responses—of a secular liberal and of a Catholic—might seem to be entirely predictable, but the observations of other critics serve to complicate the pattern. Even among those writing from a Catholic position we find contradictions. Christopher Hollis and A. A. DeVitis praise the work highly; Sean O'Faolain and Donat O'Donnell damn it. Indeed, judgments of this novel have frequently depended on a critic's view either of the nature of its religious commitment or of the relation between its satire and its sentiment. Such writers as Edmund Wilson and Charles J. Rolo feel that Waugh's commitment to Catholicism has been so complete as to distort the nature of reality; and they assert that the dilution of his satire has been catastrophic. Sean O'Faolain, from a totally different perspective, lends support to this view; he argues that in *Brideshead* Waugh has failed to universalize his art, because, in abandoning his satirical detachment, he has given "an institutional treatment" to his theme.[4] On the other hand, both DeVitis, an American admirer, and the reviewer in the *Tablet* (the English Jesuit publication) regarded *Brideshead* as a great book because they believed that it *was* apologetic.[5] Christopher Hollis and the reviewer for the *Catholic World* claimed, to the contrary, that *Brideshead* "is in no way a work of apologetics."[6]

A novel which has provoked such diverse views deserves consideration. It may be an imperfect work; it can scarcely be a vapid one. Since the apologetic nature of the work is an issue, we should, before analyzing the effects of the subordination of satire to romance, determine whether Evelyn Waugh's vision has given life a form it does not have.

In honesty to the novel, we must note at once that if by "apology" we mean a systematic and reasoned defense of a theological system, then *Brideshead* is not an apology for anything. It is not a preachy book. To be sure, the Catholicism of the Flytes is sometimes discussed. But, if we turn to the longest discussion of a theological nature in the novel, one provoked by Bridey's insistence that his dying father must receive Extreme Unction, we find not didacticism but, instead, satire. The course of the conversation proves that most of the family are confused about the issue. Ryder speaks:

> I wish someone would explain to me . . . quite what the significance of these sacraments is. Do you mean that if he dies alone he goes to hell, and that if the priest puts oil on him—"
>
> "Oh, it's not the oil," said Cordelia, "that's to heal him."
>
> "Odder still—well whatever it is the priest does—that he then goes to heaven? Is that what you believe?"
>
> Cara then interposed: "I think my nurse told me, someone did anyway, that if the priest got there before the body was cold it was all right. That's so, isn't it?"

After this amusing confusion has been cleared up, and after, as Ryder tells us, Brideshead had explained the sacrament "at some length," Ryder again speaks:

> "Let's get this clear. . . . He has to make an act of will; he has to be contrite and wish to be reconciled; is that right? But only God knows whether he has really made an act of will; the priest can't tell; and if there isn't a priest there, and he makes the act of will alone, that's as good as if there were a priest. And it's quite possible that the will may still be working when a man is too weak to make any outward sign of it; is that right? He may be lying, as though for dead, and willing all the time, and being reconciled, and God understands that; is that right?"
>
> "More or less," said Brideshead.
>
> "Well, for heaven's sake," I said, "what is the priest for?"

No one answers Ryder's question. Later he tells Julia:

> "There were four of you. . . . Cara didn't know the first thing it was about, and may or may not have believed it; you knew a bit and didn't believe a word; Cordelia knew about as much and believed it madly; only poor Bridey knew and believed, and I thought he made a pretty poor show when it came to explaining."

Over this entire scene Waugh has cast his satirical irony; the scene exists for novelistic rather than dogmatic reasons, since it prepares for an important event in the action (Lord Marchmain's conversion), satirizes the varied and confused nature of religious faith among these people, and indicates a significant stage in the development of Ryder's character. Waugh must surely be absolved of apologetic didacticism.

Similarly, if by "apologetic novel" we mean one that crudely or even subtly simplifies experience and glosses over certain of life's complexities so as to flatter a fixed system of belief, then again *Brideshead* cannot be classified as such a work. Had Waugh intended to suggest that Catholics are entirely sure of the essentials of their faith, as he might have had his purpose been so rosy an *apologia,* he would surely not have written such a scene as the one quoted above. Indeed, the author gives us no reason to believe that he is making a case for his Catholics qua Catholics, for the lives of the Marchmains and of Charles Ryder are not pretty ones, and their Catholicism is no easy consolation. Only Cordelia, the younger daughter, finds an honest contentment in faith. Her elder brother's religion is narrow adherence to system (which Waugh ridicules); and her mother's is resignation to suffering. The others—Lord Marchmain, Sebastian, Julia, and Ryder—know no rest.

Only if we choose to equate apologetics with the presentation of Catholics and Catholicism, through a "Catholic" vision of life, may we argue that the novel is an apology. Certainly the religious aspect of the novel has its roots in a fixed Catholic view. Eric Linklater, an admirer, has said of Evelyn Waugh: "Under his masterly talent for manipulating a story, under his skill in words and dextrous portrayal of character, under his keen wit and lively humor, there lies a conviction as dogmatic as that of an Indian faqir or an early Christian mystic."[7] In *Helena,* which *is* an apologetic work, the dogmatic faith attributed to Waugh by Linklater does obtrude itself, permeating the satire in a way that narrows it. That intensely held faith which suffuses both satire and romance in *Brideshead* leads, in that work, neither to didacticism nor to untruthful distortion nor to propaganda for the sake of

Riverside City College Library
Riverside, California

religious apology. As a matter of fact, Waugh has criticized Graham Greene's *The End of the Affair* as "too emphatically sectarian" and has objected to T. S. Eliot's *Cocktail Party* on the grounds that it gives the impression that the Anglican church is a "secret society."[8] At his best, apparently Evelyn Waugh would not believe that an artist should adopt an apologetic motive.

What quality does *Brideshead Revisited* exude, however, that impels Charles J. Rolo, who sees elsewhere in Waugh a "core of tragic awareness," to speak of elements in the book which he finds "trashy," "bigoted and rancorous," and to condemn the author's "obsessive and disgusting" snobbery?[9] And why does so sensitive a writer as Sean O'Faolain tell us that the novel lacks any universal validity? These judgments are not to be dismissed; they point to an inescapable limitation of the novelist's vision. If we grant that *Brideshead* is no mere work of apology, if we grant that its purpose is pre-eminently aesthetic rather than didactic, and if, as surely we must, we grant a writer the choice of a Catholic view of life, how do we account for the fact that *Brideshead* does not fulfill the promise of its brilliant satirical opening? I believe that Sean O'Faolain is illuminating on this point when he suggests that "the theme . . . is universally valid; the treatment is not."[10] Perhaps an exploration of Waugh's "treatment," which depends upon the relation between his satire and his values, will pinpoint the reason for the failure.

Brideshead Revisited is elaborately architectonic, as are other later Waugh novels. Subtitled *The Sacred and Profane Memories of Captain Charles Ryder,* the novel begins in the profane modern world and ends in the sacristy of the chapel at Brideshead. In the prologue and the epilogue, which represent the present, we find the novel's most sustained satire. As the bitterly ironic prologue opens, Charles Ryder, a captain in the British Army during World War II, is shifted from one army camp to a second locale. Arriving at night, he does not discover until morning that his new headquarters are the baroque country seat of the Flytes. This discovery moves Charles in Book I to memories of his undergraduate days and of his warm friendship with Sebastian; and in Book II, wherein Sebastian, Lord Marchmain, and Julia are all drawn back to their faith by the urgency of God's will, to memories of his love affair with Lady Julia. Book I takes place in the middle twenties and Book II in the late thirties; the intervening years are sketched in so that continuity, in the chronological sense at least, is not impaired. In the epilogue, surrounded by the "sudden frost" of the modern age, Ryder enters the chapel at Brideshead, where he is revivified by the sight of a "small red light," the sacristy lamp, signifying to him the redemptive survival of faith in a pagan world. The prologue and the epilogue are something more than a mechanical use of the frame technique; they are not merely a device for setting off the memories, but a means of expressing Waugh's emotional attitude toward the past and his satirical view of the present.

Waugh's satirical-ironic projection of a sordid present against the rich traditions of the past is strikingly effective. The landscape of the prologue, bringing into relief the traditional values which Waugh associates with Brideshead, has symbolic force. The first army camp, "a fringe of drift-wood above high-water mark," stands in the midst of a hideous landscape upon which the ugly urban "territory of housing estates and cinemas" is encroaching. Waugh describes ivy supporting "part of what had once been the walls of a fruit garden," and he depicts "half an acre of mutilated old trees." Soon there would be "no farmhouse, no wall, no apple trees. Already half a mile of concrete road lay between bare clay banks." As if this ugliness were not enough, across the road lies the municipal lunatic asylum, where sauntering and skipping madmen, "the undisputed heirs-at-law of a century of progress," may be seen.

But it is Hooper, the subaltern, who is the principal object of satire in the prologue. He has become for Ryder "a symbol . . . of young England" in a time of frost. Lazy, incompetent, without allegiance, this young man "observed the universe" from an "enveloping fog." In fact, Hooper is depressingly lower class. Moreover, a respecter of efficiency but "no romantic," he has no real sense of the past. Ryder says of Hooper, mingling satirical irony with nostalgia,

> He had not as a child ridden with Rupert's horse or sat among the camp fires at Xanthus-side; at the age when my eyes were dry to all save poetry . . . Hooper had wept often, but never for Henry's speech on St. Crispin's Day, not for the epitaph at Thermopylae. The history they had taught him had few battles in it but, instead, a profusion of detail about humane legislation and recent industrial change.

Poor, wretched Hooper is another heir of a century of progress, that dread force which the satirist despises.

In the epilogue the threat of destruction posed by the forces of the modern age (as Waugh sees it) encroaches, ironically, on Brideshead, which is taken over by the army as a training center. Ryder's commanding officer surveys the "exquisite, man-made landscape," which Ryder has described as "sequestered," "enclosed," and "embraced in a single, winding valley." The officer then comments: "The valley has great potentialities for an assault course and mortar range." And when Ryder enters the house, overwhelmed by his memories of its baroque grandeur, he finds the ground floor emptied; despite the boarding which had been used to cover the walls, the troops have managed to destroy a great fireplace, to desecrate the wall paintings (Ryder's own) in "one prettily groined" room, and to deface the *chinoiserie* of the vast room in which Lord Marchmain chose to die.

Into the great Italian fountain on the terrace "all the drivers throw their cigarette-ends and the remains of . . . sandwiches." Waugh, with the assurance of a mature artist and a mordant satirist, has lifted these details from the level of fact: he has transformed them into images of pain and disgust.

For all these depressing satirical contrasts of the prologue and epilogue, however, and for all the pleasing parallels of several returns to faith, which we find in the body of the novel, the structure of *Brideshead* is not a success. A brief examination of the organization of the two major divisions may provide an explanation of this failure. Book I, composed of eight chapters, contains 201 pages; Book II, having five chapters, occupies 116 pages. So the first book of *Brideshead* is well over half again as long as the second book. The first 148 pages of Book I recount the Oxford days of Sebastian and Charles; the rest of Book I (excepting Chapter Seven, which is devoted entirely to Julia) is concerned with Sebastian's flight from his family. But in Book II Sebastian is spoken of only twice at any length, and does not otherwise appear. Though Waugh, in Chapter Seven of Book I, prepares for Julia's emergence in the next book, he has, with a nostalgic sense of loss and regret that is scarcely touched by the kind of satire which deflates Guy Crouchback's return to adolescence, expended himself more on the Oxford section than on Ryder's crucial love affair with Julia. To make matters worse, Sebastian, who has dominated the first section, is eclipsed almost completely in the second. Is it possible that *Brideshead* has what Henry James called a "misplaced middle," that having extended himself in sentimentally re-creating the glories of a vanished past and particularly of youth, Waugh then scanted what ought really to be the center of the novel, the religious conflict engendered by the love of Julia and Ryder? Perhaps Waugh himself answered this question when he revised *Brideshead* (1960), and divided the original two books into three, apparently in an attempt to emphasize Julia's role and to subordinate the Sebastian-Oxford part to the whole.

More disturbing even than the structural flaw of *Brideshead* is the novelist's tendency so to romanticize experience that his tone degenerates into sentimentality. Nowhere is this tendency more pronounced than in the Julia-Ryder love affair, a relationship which provokes one purple passage after another. There is no satire, for example, in this typical exchange between the two:

> "Do you remember," said Julia, in the tranquil lime-scented evening, "Do you remember the storm?"
>
> "The bronze doors banging."
>
> "The roses in the cellophane."
>
> "The man who gave the 'get-together' party and was never seen again."
>
> "Do you remember how the sun came out on our last evening just as it is today?"

The contrast between the superficial glossiness of this dialogue, exchanged by romanticized and sentimentalized adulterers, and the brilliant satirical suggestion of aridity and futility in the conversations between Adam Fenwick-Symes and Nina Blount, or between Brenda and Tony Last, could not be more striking.

The consequences of the subordination of satire to sentiment are particularly evident in the point of view—that of the first-person narrator, Charles Ryder—from which Waugh has chosen to present the novel. This fictional device, whatever its merits, has also its dangers. Not only has the first-person narrator contributed to the structural defect, but his presence has nearly banished from the novel the objective, ironic, satirical detachment which had hitherto distinguished Waugh's art. In *Brideshead,* Waugh is totally committed to his hero's, and his own, strengths—a love of the past, a sense of beauty, a moral awareness of the sterility of much contemporary life. But Waugh is also committed to Ryder's weaknesses—snobbery, smugness, narrowness of sympathy, and superficial idealizations.

Through the character of Anthony Blanche, a grotesque who is a master of invective and the most brilliant satirical touch in the novel, Waugh does flash, for a moment, a bitter, ironic spotlight on his characters. To Blanche, Sebastian as a schoolboy was "a little bitch," as a young man "a little insipid," not "very well endowed in the Top Storey." Julia, Blanche says, is "a fiend—a passionless, acquisitive, intriguing, ruthless killer." Lady Marchmain, the "Reinhardt nun," he calls a "vampire." This splendid invective is poured out, however, by a character who, though he is amusing, could be charitably described as decadent; assuredly he is not reliable.

The reader, confronted with the claims Ryder makes for Sebastian and Julia, must come away from the novel with a sense of uneasiness. Ryder speaks of his college friend in terms of love, wisdom, and even of the Beatific Vision; but Sebastian is far less conspicuous for intelligence, depth of perception, and generosity than he is for his undeniable charm. And despite Ryder's adulation of Julia's renaissance beauty, her patience, her suffering, she does not emerge as a character of any real depth. Is she not the earlier Waugh heroine, plus Roman Catholicism and great wealth, now viewed through the mists of sentiment? In fact, she bears some close resemblances to Michael Arlen's famous heroine, even to the green hat and the sentimental admirer.

The extravagance in the encomia heaped upon the Flytes parallels a certain petty smugness in Ryder's satirical evaluation of others. Take the scene in which he dines with Julia's fiancé, Rex Mottram, at a particularly choice French restaurant, unknown hitherto by the obtuse politician, on "soup of *oseille,* a sole quite simply cooked in a white wine sauce, a *caneton à la presse,* a lemon soufflé," to which he adds, "at the last minute, fearing that the whole thing was too simple for Rex . . . *caviare aux blinis.*" As for wine, he allows Mottram to give him "a bottle of Montrachet, then at its prime, and, with the duck, a Clos de Bère of 1904." The scene which follows has its amusing elements, for the man who is too crude, too insensitive, to know the *real* thing, but who thinks that he does, is fair game for the satirist; however, the scene is also laced with a rather offensive snobbery, for, as course succeeds course and wine, wine, Ryder continues to congratulate himself on the superiority of his taste to Rex's. Mottram is a boor, because he is just not one of the initiated: after all, how could a *Canadian* upstart be expected to know? At the end of the meal, over brandy and cigars, the two relax. Mottram "sat back at peace with the world; I too," Ryder tells us with egregious self-satisfaction, "was at peace in another world than his." It would seem that in scenes such as this one Waugh has had to surrender the objectivity of his satirical intelligence.

The failure to objectify the allegiances of his hero (and fictional point of view) obtains even more glaringly in the ironic contrast between the present and Hooper, on the one hand, and, on the other, the traditions of the past and Brideshead. Donat O'Donnell is moved to exclaim, "Is Lord Marchmain's soul more valuable than Hooper's? To say in so many words that it was would be heresy, but *Brideshead Revisited* almost seems to imply that the wretched Hooper has no soul at all."[11] Indeed, to view objectively the imperfections for which Hooper is satirized—a low level of intelligence, a naïve respect for "modern efficiency," a personal incompetence, a dissociation from the heroic past—together with the collective sins of the Brideshead and Charles Ryder—innumerable adulteries, apostasies, alcoholism, spiritual pride, and probably sexual perversion—is to conclude that Ryder has forgotten that hell and purgatory have circles and circles.

Albert Camus' analysis of the act of rebellion may illuminate Evelyn Waugh's development. The early satirical novels sprang from the kind of rejection of man's condition which has led some men to nihilism, others to modern forms of totalitarianism, and Waugh, an artist, to a destructive satirical technique which withheld assent. But, as Camus suggests, rebellion to be fruitful cannot be complete; if it is creative, it limits itself. As the rebel rejects what he despises, he also—and simultaneously—affirms something superior to what he repudiates, in the name of all other men, with whom he senses a bond of unity. Differing from the earlier works, *Brideshead* springs not only from rejection but also from assent, from acceptance of a Catholic framework which has been confused with a class-view. *Brideshead* makes no universal affirmation. Although it satirically repudiates what is vile to its author and emotionally affirms a unity he had never suggested before, it does not achieve that fruitful tension between the "yes" and "no" of rebellion. The satirical rejection of the young Hooper, of Father Mackay, and of Rex Mottram—in short of the middle and lower orders of society—is complete. Waugh can find no real grounds for sympathy with them. The terrible weaknesses of the Marchmain family are fully developed, but so many excuses are made for them (which is not done for the nonupper-class, minor characters, nearly all of whom are satirized), so extravagant are Ryder's claims for them, so romanticized is their class position, so much nostalgia is lavished on the life they were able to lead before the war, so many indications are given of their exclusive right to consideration, so much of Ryder's smugness and self-satisfaction permeates the whole, that the novel seems to accept Brideshead and everything it entails totally and at the expense of all other beings.

But the last words on *Brideshead* really belong to Evelyn Waugh. In the preface to the revised edition—itself a comment on the original—Waugh left no doubt at all as to his dissatisfaction with this work, which had damaged his reputation at the same time that it brought fame. He frankly admitted that its "rhetorical and ornamental language" had become "distasteful" to him. Indeed, in the very act of offering the revised novel to a new generation of readers, as "a souvenir of the Second War rather than of the twenties or of the thirties with which it ostensibly deals," he seemed to be unconvinced that he had greatly improved it. And, it must be said, the revised novel is not a success. Although Waugh did curb some of the excesses of the original, he did not obliterate its grosser qualities. (A complete reworking of the second half of the original would have been necessary to do so.) So it was not surprising to find Waugh returning in his most recent novel once again to the subject of *Brideshead.* The grotesque and fruity Ludovic, who was jotting down satirical aphorisms throughout *Officers and Gentlemen,* emerges in *Unconditional Surrender* as the author of a "gorgeous almost gaudy tale of romance." Unknown to him, writes Waugh, half a dozen other English novelists were also "composing or preparing to compose books which would turn the drab alleys of the thirties into the odorous gardens of a recent past transformed and illuminated by disordered memory and imagination." The lush and decadent product of Ludovic's melancholic imagination is a novel which ends with the lingering death of his heroine, Lady Marmaduke; her demise, a "protracted" and "ceremonious" affair, takes place in luxurious surroundings amidst the trappings of great wealth. The exquisite decline of Lady Marmaduke is thus the most telling comment on *Brideshead Revisited*: it is a delightful parody of the passing of Lord Marchmain amidst the *chinoiserie* of Brideshead House.

CHAPTER X

Helena and the Solid Chunk of Wood

IN *Brideshead Revisited* those elements of Evelyn Waugh's Catholicism—its traditionalism and its respect for order—which could most easily be assimilated by his social bias were nearly absorbed by his idealization of the life of the aristocracy and by the sentimentality which may accompany it. In *Helena,* the second of Waugh's Catholic novels, the rationalistic element of the novelist's religion dominates; baroque lushness has been restrained. The satirical element has once again emerged in full strength. Never as brilliant as the best of *Brideshead, Helena* is, nevertheless, highly regarded by some of Waugh's admirers. Frederic J. Stopp considers it the "peak" of the novelist's later career, and Aubrey Menen, seconding Waugh's own judgment, believes it to be a "masterpiece."[1]

The felicities of Waugh's version of the life of St. Helena, mother of Constantine the Great and legendary discoverer of the true cross, are many. Waugh's prose, which is supple, allusive, ripe, is also restrained enough to avoid the excesses of *Brideshead.* Handling his only historical novel with the dexterity of a polished craftsman, Waugh has wisely avoided false archaism and flat neutrality of diction. The characters speak the language Waugh's characters have always spoken, that mannered and highly stylized selection from upper-class speech which is both amusing and, despite its artificiality, convincing. Though Helena's "Oh, what sucks!" and "What a blow out!" may have pained many readers, they do not violate the spirit of a work that constantly mingles gravity and satirical irreverence.

Another of the charms of *Helena* is Waugh's clever reshaping of traditional legendary material to create satirical effects. We experience a pleasant shock of recognition when, a moment after Helena's father, King Coel, roars for mead and music, "only the three strings and the pipe," we understand both that a nursery rhyme has been given new life and also that King Cole was really a loud and pompous old fellow. It has suited Waugh's purpose to reject that version of Helena's legend which identifies her as the concubine of Constantius, possibly elevated from some lowly station at Drepanum, and to imagine her as a princess of Roman Britain. He entertains us, in a parody of the farfetched etymologies of the *Legenda Aurea,* with a fanciful etymology of "Stabularia," a name which might have associated Helena with a humbler origin than the one Waugh has given her. Helena indulges in a fantasy in which she imagines herself a high-spirited horse; when she first meets Constantius, she submits, in her fantasy, to his will as her rider. Later, when Constantius, who feels the effects of last night's banquet, encounters her in the stable, she is wearing a bridle. He asks:

> "What do you do besides hang about the stables?"
>
> "Oh, I'm still being educated. I'm the King's daughter you know and we Britons think a lot of education. What's your name?"
>
> "Constantius. What's yours?"
>
> "Helena. Green-faced Constantius."
>
> "Helena the ostler."
>
> And so these names, "Chlorus" and "Stabularia," lightly blown, drifted away into the dawn and settled at last among the pages of history.

All this gently satirical playfulness may be engaging, the

puritan conscience protests, but is it not rather light? Waugh's handling of this legend would suggest that it is possible to be at once playful and serious. After Helena's invention of the cross, for example, she learns that Constantine has taken one of the nails which supposedly pierced the body of Christ and had it forged into a snaffle for his horse. "When Helena heard this she was at first a little taken back. But presently she smiled, giggled, and was heard to utter the single, enigmatic word 'stabularia.'" Mr. Waugh is not merely trifling; he is amusing us, of course, but he is also shaping the legendary material, at the very moment that it seems most lightly satiric, to express a meaningful theme—the operation, as in *Brideshead,* of God's providence in a pagan world.

Actually, the apparent playfulness of the satire in *Helena* is deceptive. Many of the satirical touches are based upon the incongruous association of modern diction, attitudes, or manners with the customs of the late Roman Empire. As the ladies of Coel's court rise from their private repast during the King's feast honoring the visiting Constantius, Helena's aunt asserts, "We won't go in quite yet. The gentlemen have just gone to be sick." On the surface, this detail seems little more than an ingenious and incidental thrust at the excesses of a decadent civilization. But the casualness is only apparent; Waugh has carefully opposed to this feast, which Helena anticipates as the novel opens, the feast day of the Church, Easter Sunday, the long-awaited day on which Helena, as the novel draws to a close, discovers the cross. The ironic contrast between the two feasts—one marked by the tiresome boasts of Coel, the political maneuvering of Constantius, the excesses of gluttony and drunkenness, and the visits to the vomitorium, the other, by a spiritual event of the greatest significance which follows days of fasting—could not be more deliberate.

The deliberateness of the satire in *Helena* indicates the overt apologetic nature of the work. In *The Age of Constan-*

tine the Great Jacob Burckhardt observed that the scattered notices concerning Helena, Crispus, and others would allow a writer "with a certain quality of pragmatism and a certain quality of imagination" to write a romance which would be "very interesting and at the same time totally untrue from beginning to end."[2] Given the paucity of verifiable historical documents and the legendary quality of most of the material concerning Helena and Constantine, a writer could choose to do nearly anything that would please both his imagination and his sense of fact. Though it would be possible, on historical grounds, to dispute Waugh's satirical attack on Constantine as a corrupt and decadent neurotic, a semipagan who used Christianity merely to flatter his own monstrous vanity and to quiet his confused pagan fears, the historical accuracy of this work is not really an important consideration. As Waugh points out in the preface, *Helena* is neither history nor archeology, but a novel. Nevertheless, the particular slant Waugh gives to the satirical details shaped by imagination and by his sense of fact raises a number of questions. Why are so many villains, knaves, and fools satirized in the novel? Why does Waugh impute honorable motives and grant a measure of dignity only to Helena and Pope Sylvester? What does the satire apologize for, and what aesthetic consequence derives from the domination of the apologetic motive?

Perhaps a passage from the novel, in which we see a clash between Helena and the Emperor Constantine, who is a grotesque, may provide the basis for answers to these questions. In this scene, wherein Constantine, who is exposed to ridicule, defends himself against his mother, who has assumed the role of ingénue, we can discern both the central theme of the novel and the apologetic motive which informs the satire:

"Have I explained myself? Do you see now how cruelly unfair it is to compare me with Nero? . . . All I need is to be understood and appreciated. I know what I'll do," he continued, brightening. "If you promise not to be angry with me any more I'll show you Something Very Special."

He led her to the sacristy that opened from the great hall of the palace. He called for keys and with his hands opened a cupboard; inside stood a tall parcel swathed in silk. A sacristan offered assistance. "Go away," Constantine said. "No one is allowed to touch this except myself. Very few have ever seen it."

With eager clumsiness he unwrapped his exhibit and then stood clear, posing grandly with it in his right hand.

The thing was the size and shape of a military standard. Its head formed a Latin cross, gold-plated. Above was a jewelled wreath of elaborate design and in the center of the wreath a jewelled monogram, the sacred XP. From the crossbar hung a banner of purple satin richly embroidered and gemmed, bearing . . . a motto . . . and a series of delicately stitched medallion portraits.

"What on earth have you got there?" asked Helena.

"Can't you *see*. It's *It*, my Labarum."

Helena studied this magnificent piece of arts and crafts with growing bewilderment. "You don't mean to say that you carried *that* into action at the Milvian Bridge."

"Of course. In this sign I conquered."

"But, Constantine, the story as I always heard it was that you had a vision on the eve of the battle and that then and there you changed the markings on the troops' shields and had the armourer knock up your own standard in the shape of the cross."

"Certainly. This is it."

"And you had this made in camp."

"Yes. Isn't it interesting?"

"But it must have taken years to make."

"Two or three hours, I assure you. The jewellers were inspired. Everything was miraculous that day."

"And whose are the portraits?"

"My own and my children's."

"But, my dear boy, they weren't all born then."

"I tell you it was a miracle," said Constantine huffily. "If you're not interested I'll put it away."

Most apparent here, of course, is the personal conflict between the hardheaded simplicity of the mother and the deluded pomposity of the son, whose ridiculous vanity dissolves for him the distinction between fact and figment, reality and illusion. The conflict, however, is more than personal; the novel also demonstrates the clash between the logical, rule-of-thumb Catholicism of Evelyn Waugh and the obscurantism which he regards as its enemy.

Helena, who embodies her creator's rationalism, is always the tough-minded, pragmatic, no-nonsense English aristocrat, the standard by which all the objects of satire are measured. When she first encounters the varieties of religious mysticism which pervade the Empire, the "secret meetings, passwords, initiations, trances, and extraordinary sensations" to which the ladies of the provincial center are addicted, she asks, "It's all bosh isn't it?" As Constantius attempts to explain the cult of Mithras to her, she listens attentively to myth of bull, cave, and sun god; but then, with the same disconcerting directness which later exposed the Labarum as a fraud, asks "*Where* did it happen?" Later, attending a lecture given by her former tutor, Marcias, a Gnostic who has become "the latest thing in Higher thought," she giggles at his talk of what is beyond space and time. Again, she wants to know where and when. Rejecting all Oriental and mystical "bosh," she finally does find that Lactantius, her son's tutor, can answer her questions:

> "Tell me, Lactantius, this god of yours. If I asked you when and where he could be seen, what would you say?"
>
> "I should say that as a man he died two hundred and seventy eight years ago in the town called Aelia Capitolina in Palestine."
>
> "Well, that's a straight answer anyway. How do you know?"
>
> "We have the accounts written by witnesses. Besides there is the living memory of the Church."

Just as in *Brideshead Revisited* spiritual turmoil is avoided, so in *Helena* the most intense religious experience is glossed over. Of Helena's conversion we learn little more than that "She was one seed in a vast germination." While Waugh assumes miraculous intervention to account for Helena's invention of the cross, this aspect of her legend does not really interest him. In an essay he states his heroine's distinction:

> She was asserting in sensational form a dogma that was in danger of neglect. Power was shifting. In the academies of the Eastern and South-Eastern Mediterranean sharp, sly minds were everywhere looking for phrases and analogies to reconcile the new, blunt creed for which men had died, with the ancient speculations which had beguiled their minds, and with the occult rites which for generations spiced their logic.[3]

Waugh's Helena, irritated by all those fools and knaves who chatter about hypostatic union and by her son's superstitious veneration of a phony "miracle," decides that "there's a solid chunk of wood waiting for them to have their silly heads knocked against" and that she must find it. Helena's unique claim to sainthood, as Waugh envisions her, is her blunt assertion that the wood of the cross "states a fact," that is, the historicity of Christianity and thus the redemption of man in time. The problem of whether the essentials of Christianity rest upon "fact" and bear no reference to abstruse metaphysical speculations need not concern us here. What does seem inescapable is the conclusion that in *Helena* the satire is the instrument of apology, and that the satire apologizes particularly for Evelyn Waugh's version of Catholicism.

To deny that a work may be both apologetic in nature and effectively satirical would be idle. A certain quality of intolerance in Waugh's rationalistic Catholicism manifests itself, however, in this novel. Anything that might obscure the open altar and the reasonable clarity of the tradition that Helena and Sylvester adhere to is, in Waugh's mind, "hazy and obscure nonsense." Therefore, those who differ with Helena are scoundrels, or worse. Most of them belong to the realm of grotesque satire: Marcias, the Gnostic, is a eunuch and a fraud, at home only "in the void which he made his chilly home"; Constantine, who mingles paganism and Christianity, is a pitiful example of power without grace, a near madman in a green wig; Fausta, an Arian heretic, is a vulgar, meretricious, power-hungry, adulterous "advanced" thinker; Constantius, who becomes an initiate of the lower levels of the Mithraic cult, is nearly soulless; Eusebius of Nicomedia, another "progressive" Arianizer, is "creepy-crawly"; Eusebius of Caesaria, who was hostile to Western domination of the Church, is a former apostate and perhaps even one of those who acted as an informer during the persecution.

Even those uninfected by mysticism, whose rationalism has led them to different conclusions from Waugh's, do not escape censure. These figures are satirized by means of invective. The Wandering Jew, who appears to Helena in a dream vision, is a free-thinker with "crocodile" eyes, tolerant of all religions because indifferent to all; he leaves the mark of a goat's hoof in the earth and is made responsible for all the false relics circulated throughout Christian history. Waugh also slips in an unnecessary invective attack on the historian Edward Gibbon, who is identified with an ape and described as "a false historian with the mind of Cicero or Tacitus and the soul of an animal." The direction of this satire, with its contemporary references to mystics of one kind or another, to those (such as Lawrence or Huxley) of eclectic and personal vision, to the unorthodox, to the secular, suggests the intensity of Waugh's faith and his apprehension for its future. It also suggests some want of charity.

In *Helena,* as in *Brideshead Revisited,* other elements of Waugh's generally conservative attitude tend to mingle with the conservatism of his religious views. There are, for example, amusing and oblique satirical onslaughts on functional architecture and nonrepresentational sculpture. On other occasions, however, satirical obliquity will not serve, and Waugh becomes didactic. Such is the case when Helena, having a serious attack of prescience, describes a terrible dream of the future: "... people may forget their loyalty to their kings and emperors and take power for themselves. Instead of letting one victim bear this frightful curse they will take it all on themselves, each one of them. Think of the misery of a whole world possessed of Power without Grace."

In *Helena,* Waugh has thus moved one step beyond *Brideshead;* now he not only affirms a positive value but even, like Aldous Huxley in his later work, instructs. Such direct moralizing does not exist elsewhere in Waugh's satires; and, since *Helena,* the novelist has not again attempted apologetic fiction. Despite his assertion at the time of *Brideshead* that his future novels would be concerned with "man in his relation to God,"[4] in the three Crouchback novels the religious element, at last satisfactorily related to Waugh's political conservatism, is subordinate though pervasive. Consequently, there is reason to believe that *Helena* marked one stage in a development that began in *Work Suspended* and reached its peak in the Crouchback novels. Considered now in relation to the subsequent novels, *Helena* can be seen as another effort by Waugh to adjust his satirical impulse to a less stylized, more conventional novel. It also represents a transitional phase in his continuing effort to master a satirical technique that would not merely destroy but also create value.

Part Five

THE PRESENT AGE AND THE PASSING ORDER

CHAPTER XI

To the Right

EVELYN Waugh attended an exhibit of contemporary art in Paris in 1929. Examining the nonrepresentational canvases, he was particularly amused by the juxtaposition of a Picabia and an Ernst. Of the two paintings, hanging side by side, he observed:

> These two abstract pictures, the one so defiant and chaotic, probing with such fierce intensity into every crevice and convolution of negation, the other so delicately poised, so impossibly tidy, discarding so austerely every accident, however agreeable, that could tempt disorder, seemed between them to typify the continual conflict of modern society.[1]

This statement is no idle speculation. It points to the striking fact that Evelyn Waugh has always been conscious of the antinomies of chaos and order and has felt them to be particularly pronounced in the modern world.

I have indicated earlier that in his "negative" satires Waugh focused his attention on the disorders of modern society, but that beginning with *Brideshead Revisited* he also sought to adumbrate a religious value which might bring order into chaos. I also pointed out that he has mingled and confused his social-political allegiance, another principle of order, with his Roman Catholicism. The course of Waugh's political development and the nature of his political orientation have evoked hostility and resentment among critics, reviewers, and readers. The constant accusation of "snobbery," for example, reflects these feelings. But such hostility has not served to illuminate Waugh's politics. It seems advisable, therefore, to explore both the course of Evelyn Waugh's political development and the element of conservatism in his works.

We might scoff at the assertion that the contrasting paintings—the Picabia and the Ernst—express the continual conflict between negative chaos and extreme order, which Waugh held to be typical of the modern world. After all, we might ask, when has the social life of man not manifested itself as a conflict between order and disorder? It has been observed, perhaps wisely, that there is no bad time like the present. Yet it may also be said, with reason, that even if our century has not exhibited intense and extreme conflicts between these opposites, poets, novelists, and dramatists have *believed* that it has. Indeed, haunted by the spectacle of negation and chaos which they saw around them, many men of letters, in revulsion, have embraced extreme systems of order. Writing in 1923, long before the events which may now appear as the most appalling of the century, Aldous Huxley stated that "other epochs have witnessed disasters, have had to suffer disillusionment, but in no century have the disillusionments followed on one another's heels with such unintermittent rapidity as in the twentieth."[2] Literary men have reacted to this disenchantment by repudiating those conditions and institutions which they deemed responsible for, or involved in, the disorder of the age.

One of the principal complaints among British writers has been political. The literary history of the first half of the century is studded with major and minor artists who, dismayed by the chaos of democratic capitalism and rejecting what they believed to be the direction of their society, assumed a political position to the extreme right, or even, in some cases, completely repudiated the very traditions of Western democracy. The terrible irony of this development is that in the name of order men have submitted their minds and souls to some of the most destructive and disorderly tyrannies of history, or to private and less dreadful visions of order which, if realized, would surely lead only to servitude for the vast majority.

Popular mythology often depicts communism as the most insidious and pervasive political influence on the intelligentsia during the second and third decade of this century. In England, however, at least as many important writers were moved to positions far to the right of the Tory party, and even to fascism, as were attracted to communism. To be sure, W. H. Auden, Stephen Spender, and Day Lewis flirted briefly with the Communist party; Sean O'Casey joined it, more or less; Hugh MacDiarmid joined it, for a while at least, and remained faithful to the cause; Christopher Caudwell, the Marxist critic, joined the Communist party and died for it in Spain. On the other hand, G. K. Chesterton, Hilaire Belloc, George Bernard Shaw, William Butler Yeats, D. H. Lawrence, T. S. Eliot, Wyndham Lewis, Ezra Pound, Roy Campbell, and Evelyn Waugh—all excepting Shaw hostile to communism—were drawn to extreme rightist positions.

Among those rightist men of letters adorned in the robes of contemporary neoclassicism, fascism found its most convinced exponents. T. S. Eliot—classicist, royalist, and Anglo-Catholic—as editor of the *Criterion* indicated his disapproval of democracy, his respect for Oswald Mosley's Fascists and for the *Action française,* but whether through lack of candor, as Kathleen Nott has suggested, or lack of enthusiasm, he never actually committed himself to any kind of fascism.[3] However, the other "classical" writers—Ezra Pound, Wyndham Lewis, and Roy Campbell—may be described best as Fascists. Pound's obsessive hatred of capitalism ("usury") and his contempt for the masses led him to support the corporate state of Mussolini. And a more coherent thinker than Pound, Wyndham Lewis, damned the confusing flux of modern life, the party system, the democratic herd, liberalism, and a good many other things he despised, and put the case for order, authority, and control. In consequence of his respect for order and restraint, Lewis (who only began to recant in 1939) supported Mussolini's invasion of Abyssinia, the cause of Franco in Spain, and the Nazism of Hitler. In *Snooty Baronet* (1932) the Lewis persona, "Snooty," found it easy to establish contact with the bullfighter Rob McPhail (who stood for Lewis' friend Roy Campbell). Two words alone were needed, "Snooty" tells us: " 'Mussolini!' I said. 'Action!' " Campbell, another hater of humanitarianism and democracy, has described the triumphant Franco lifting "three fallen centuries from the slime"; he probably summed up the rightist attitude of contemporary neoclassicists when he wrote, "Of Liberty or Freedom they've enough / Who've learned to dread the nambypamby stuff."[4]

Certain resemblances and parallels would seem to associate the political attitudes of Evelyn Waugh with those of such satirists as Lewis and Campbell. During the thirties, Waugh openly supported both Mussolini and Franco. Like Lewis, he has ridiculed respect for the primitive and has argued that the entire West suffers from an inferiority complex with respect to Negroes. He has also agreed with Lewis in condemning, as a manifestation of that inferiority complex, contemporary interest in jazz. In 1936, when Lewis argued that England, by supporting sanctions against Italy, was sponsoring Negro aggression, Waugh took a similar line and held that "the Socialists of Europe . . . nearly succeeded in precipitating world war in defence of an archaic African despotism." In that same year, when Lewis was denouncing freedom of the press as nothing more than freedom for "*intellectual* Jack-the-Rippers," Waugh, following up his satirical attack—in *Remote People* and *Waugh in Abyssinia*—on the irresponsibility of the press, observed that it is purely ironic to refer to a private press system as "free." He indicated his regret, moreover, that "no responsibility curbs" the press's "extravagance." When Waugh announced at the beginning of his career that "Freedom produces sterility," he anticipated Roy Campbell's doggerel detraction of "Liberty" and "Freedom." And Waugh's ridicule of "the peevish whinny of the nonconformist conscience" which sympathized with the Abyssinian "barbarians" during the Italian invasion is separated from Campbell's description of humanitarianism as "protestantism gone bad," sympathizing with "the Jew against the Christian, the black against the white, the servant against the master," only by Campbell's more violent invective.

Because Waugh took such stands as these during the thirties, it became possible to identify him with fascism. Dame Rose Macaulay labeled *Waugh in Abyssinia* a "fascist tract," and Donat O'Donnell asserted that "If England had developed a Fascism of its own, a 'Cavalier' type as distinct from the Jacobin type of Peguy, this Fascism would have had no more fanatical supporter than Mr. Waugh."[5]

"Fascist tract" is probably an apt description of *Waugh in Abyssinia,* but Donat O'Donnell's hypothesis does Evelyn Waugh an injustice. Those attitudes which seem to parallel the ideas of Lewis and Campbell indicate not that Waugh was ever a convinced Fascist or that he is another child of T. E. Hulme, but that, moving in the same direction as these other rightists, he shared some unsavory attitudes with them. Waugh's political extravagances, disturbing to many reasonable men, are more closely akin to those of Hilaire Belloc or Yeats than to those of the most extreme English "classicists." Never a consistent political thinker or a shaper of immense symbolistic structures, Waugh was moved by the strength of disgust and prejudice to adopt positions which did him little honor. A connection exists, undoubtedly, between his Catholicism and his support for Mussolini and Franco, but the connection is not that Catholicism and fascism are inevitably allied, as some would have it. If this alliance has existed in writers such as Roy Campbell, Charles Péguy, and Georges Bernanos, Catholicism has certainly led to a different political orientation in other men, such as G. K. Chesterton, Graham Greene, and Jacques Maritain. Nevertheless, the course of Waugh's political development and the whole tendency to the right among English writers of this century do illustrate one bitter truth: "Every form of contempt, if it intervenes in politics, prepares the way for, or establishes, Fascism."[6]

Certain of Waugh's nonfictional accounts of travels best demonstrate the evolution of that political conservatism which forms the basis of several satires. Before we directly approach the political Waugh who emerges in the travel books, however, we must first examine the image of himself as a man of the world which Waugh sought to create in these books. According to Frederic Stopp, *Labels* initiated a new kind of travel book: the "sophisticated" variety.[7] Certainly the image of self which Waugh projected in *Labels* was one of sophistication, of a sophistication composed of a unique blend of insouciance and irony. The Waugh who traveled in this book had a wicked sense of the grotesque; he had adopted a pose which helped him to confront and to satirize the crazy world. As in the early satires, we are led to believe that nothing could possibly shock him, not even the child who showed him "with genuine enthusiasm" the half-disembowled, mummified corpse in an Italian church, inhaled it "deeply and greedily," and recommended that he do the same.[8]

But when, in *Remote People,* the blasé wit, the sophisticated ironist, visited Africa, the significance of the pose he had adopted was revealed. As the festivities accompanying the coronation of Haile Selassie waned, Waugh found himself, one night, standing at the window of his room. He looked out upon a cluster of huts, where the natives still celebrated: "They were singing a monotonous song, clapping in time and drumming with their hands on petrol-tins. I suppose there were about ten or fifteen of them there. I stood for some time listening. I was wearing a tall hat, evening clothes and white gloves. Presently the guard woke up and blew a little trumpet. . . ." Suddenly Waugh saw the absurdity of his entire Abyssinian experience typified by that situation: his "preposterous clothes" and "the wakeful party on the other side of the stockade." The serious Evelyn Waugh, who longed for order and civilization in the midst of chaos and whose emblem was formal dress, confronted the primitive; the civilized man behind the sophisticated mask was stirred to laughter or disgust and, hence, to satire.

That the sophistication of the man of the world was not the essence of Waugh, but only an aspect, was made amply clear by his encounter with Mr. Bergebedgian, hotelkeeper at Harar. "He was an Armenian of rare character," Waugh wrote, and "I became greatly attached to him." In all of Mr. Bergebedgian's opinions Waugh "found great delight," for the Armenian "had no prejudice or scruples of race, creed, or morals of any kind." Mr. Bergebedgian was, in essence, the blasé sophisticate whose mask Waugh assumed for satirical effect. Contemplating himself by contrast to this "genuine" man of the world, Waugh wrote:

> I shall never in actual fact become a 'hard-boiled man of the world.' . . . I shall always be ill at ease with nine out of every ten people I meet. . . . I shall always find something startling and rather abhorrent in the things most other people think worth doing, and something startling in their standards of importance. . . . I shall probably be increasingly, rather than decreasingly, vulnerable to the inevitable minor injustices of life.[9]

So speaks the man of values who is a more important part of Evelyn Waugh than the pretender to worldliness.

All this seems remote from the question of political conservatism. But it is not, in very truth. One consequence of Evelyn Waugh's dual role—as the man who finds the activities of others abhorrent and as the man of the world—is the satirical tone of urbane detachment tinged with disgust which pervades *Remote People, Waugh in Abyssinia,* and such satires as *Black Mischief.* In terms of Waugh's personal political development, the combination of man of the world and man of values is no less important. When Evelyn Waugh gads about the Mediterranean, around Africa, or in Mexico, he travels *as* a man of the world. At Port Said he has "tea at the vicarage, dinner at the consulate, cocktails at Navy House." At Aden, during a brief visit, he attends "a dance at the club, a ball at the Residency, and a very convivial party given by the Sappers." At Crater, Waugh is fetched by "a smart car with a liveried Italian chauffeur" to dinner on the roof and iced *vin rosé.* On the first day in Nairobi, he taxis to the Muthaiga Club where everyone is drinking pink gin in impressive quantities; he is involved in a luncheon party and goes to the races; afterwards, at Muthaiga again, he drinks champagne from a silver cup. Then he goes off to a "very large dinner-party, taking up all one side of the ballroom at Torrs." Waugh begins the round of the fashionable estates; he picnics with a large party in the jungle; he breakfasts, when roughing it with a bachelor friend, on "grouse paste and a bottle of soda water." He visits Naivasha, where he swims in the morning, eats huge luncheons, and sleeps in the afternoon. He remembers the small, hot sausages his hostess served at cocktail time. Even from the political wasteland of Mexico it is possible for him to carry away memories of "a bottle of magnificent claret" and of the "good company in the Ritz bar."[10]

When the satirist managed to turn his attention from the pleasures of this fashionable whirl, he could find in the underdeveloped African nations much to amuse the man of the world but little to satisfy him, and absolutely nothing to please the man who set a high value on civilization. The period Waugh spent in Addis Ababa at the time of Haile

Selassie's coronation was, for example, a "preposterous *Alice in Wonderland* fortnight" during which reality seemed peculiarly "galvanised and translated." The entire episode was a perfect subject for the satirist's nice and subtle awareness of differences. The streets of the Ethiopian capital, described by the guidebook as "elegant and smiling," he found to be "mere stretches of waste-land between blocks of houses." The widely heralded accomplishments of the new Emperor were spurious; his subjects had little respect even for his shrewdness until European nations created his prestige by sending important representatives to the coronation ceremonies. The people of the Abyssinian Empire, at their best, were "great shaggy dogs of uncertain temper."

The ceremonies accompanying the coronation of Ras Tafari as Haile Selassie were farcical. At one, which was typical of all the festivities, workmen were still "chipping at the surrounding masonry and planting drooping palm-trees in the arid beds." When the equestrian statue, which the public obviously failed to understand, was finally unveiled, the element of farce again intervened. Folds of silk clung to the statue and "obstinately fluttered over the horse's ears and eyes."[11] The coronation ceremony itself Waugh regarded as a tangle of barbarism and sham modernity. He found no such confusion in the Ethiopian interior, however, for it seemed entirely squalid and savage. Other African nations he considered even more appalling. In Zanzibar, Waugh found that Hindu enterprise had managed to create "a mean and dirty culture"; in Uganda, a Catholic convent was the sole "island of order and sweetness in an ocean of rank barbarity"; in the Congo, no redeeming feature existed.

The alternatives to these African "nightmares" to which the civilized man might turn were Aden and Kenya, as far as Waugh was concerned. In the former (a British protectorate), English rule, he argued, had made it possible for the English colony to enjoy that leisure which is requisite to civilization and for Arab sultans to lead lives which formed "a complete parallel to the lives of the enlightened landed gentlemen of eighteenth century England." In the colony of Kenya, also, the life of the eighteenth century had been re-created. The settlers of this land, a place of "warm loveliness and breadth and generosity," had managed to "perpetuate a habit of life traditional to them, which England has ceased to accommodate—the traditional life of the English squierarchy . . . to which . . . we can as a race look back with unaffected esteem and regret." Waugh's rhetorical flourishes, as he sums up his impressions of Kenya, reveal exactly what happened in his political development during the thirties. That deeper aspect of Waugh's nature which craved stability, order, and the grace of civilization identified these qualities with the fashionable, upper-class society in which the man of the world had been able to move. It was possible for Waugh to romanticize and, indeed, to sentimentalize the life of the wealthy landowners of Kenya and to identify himself, as artist, with them. "The Kenya settlers," he wrote, "are not cranks of the kind who colonised New England, nor criminals and ne'er-do-wells of the kind who went to Australia, but perfectly normal, respectable Englishmen, out of sympathy with their own age, and for this reason linked to the artist in an unusual but very real way."[12]

The romantic Waugh, the seeker after order who wrote satires because most people in his time did not live as he imagined the aristocrats of the eighteenth century had, was led to adopt the imperialist arguments by which his friends defended their colonial position. In *Remote People* Waugh argued the absurdity of suggesting that, because Europeans have lost their belief in revealed religion and have fallen "back helplessly for moral guidance on their own tenderer feelings," at a given moment in recent history, imperialism became "wrong." In substance Waugh defended imperialism by stating that the relations between powerful nations, on the one hand, and weak, underdeveloped territories, on the other, are governed by no moral law whatsoever. Instead, one general rule applies: "... that the whole of history, from the earliest times until today, has been determined by the movements of peoples about the earth's surface." So, ironically, the man who had sought order and had satirized because he resented its absence, could justify moral anarchy and the rule of force. And Waugh was led one step further by his romantic commitment to the order of things in Kenya: he held that the reader who had spent no time in the tropics had no right to be censorious about the Englishman's sense of superiority to the natives whose lands he had colonized. Perhaps Anglo-Saxon supremacy is an irrational concept, Waugh wrote, but it is also worth considering "the possibility that there may be something valuable behind the indefensible and inexplicable assumption of superiority by the Anglo-Saxon race."[13]

By the time of *Waugh in Abyssinia,* however, no shred of ironic doubt remained. Waugh was prepared to assert, in this account of the Italian aggression, that the Abyssinians were "by any possible standards an inferior race."[14] Fascist racism? Possible, but doubtful. Waugh actually is tied to an older ideology which moves, to be sure, in the same direction as Fascist racism and often bears similar fruit. In *Remote People* and *Waugh in Abyssinia* he is reactionary in that, evoking once again the attitude of such writers of the late nineteenth century as Rudyard Kipling and W. H. Hudson, he argues that the European is entitled to carry civilization, by force if necessary, to the "lesser breeds without the Law."

In *Waugh in Abyssinia,* it must be granted, the writer's sense of the superiority of European civilization to that of Africa, the amorality of his imperialism, and the romanticism of his thirst for order do approximate the politics of fascism. Waugh has reached the ultimate consequence of contempt. This account of the Italo-Ethiopian war and of a return visit to the conquered African land is so laced with distortions, misrepresentations, and illogicalities that as serious reporting it must be discounted. *Waugh in Abyssinia* is sheer invective propaganda, unilluminated by the more subtle satirical insights of *Remote People.* The Abyssinian populace, we learn, is a "half-human rabble." The Emperor's attempted reforms are a fraud. Tafari himself is a shrewd and disingenuous manipulator of the European powers. He is, indeed, different from Count Vinci, the Italian minister, who is "cheerful, courageous, friendly and slightly mischievous," or the conquering General Graziani, who is "like the traditional conception of an English admiral, frank, humorous, and practical." The Italian case against Abyssinia has been clear from the start. Since Abyssinia could not possibly develop her own resources, "it must be done for her." Abyssinia must "put her natural resources at the disposal of the world." Might an Abyssinia placed under the protection of the League be preferable to an Abyssinia annexed to the Italian Empire? No: "An unconquered Abyssinia would never accept effective reform."[15]

At the close of this book, Waugh (being, not too surprisingly, the first non-Italian reporter admitted after the conquest) describes a visit to the great trunk-line road which the Italians were constructing from Massawa to Asmara. One of his characters in *Vile Bodies,* Nina Blount, looked down from an airplane on such a road in England and wanted to vomit; but now Waugh grows lyrical in an extended tribute to this great Italian achievement, which "brings order and fertility" to a barbarian land. Having completely suspended his satirical sense, he notes with pleasure that the Italian workmen have embellished the roadside with charming gardens, ornamental devices of colored pebbles, fasces, and heads of Mussolini. He concludes by praising the "great metalled highway," symbol of Roman accomplishment, for carrying with it "the inestimable gifts of fine workmanship and clear judgment—the two determining qualities of the human spirit, by which alone, under God, man grows and flourishes."[16]

Two years after *Waugh in Abyssinia,* Waugh declared, in a letter to the *New Statesman,* that he did not want or expect a Fascist regime in England. Even when, in the same year, he declared that if he were a Spaniard he would be fighting for General Franco, he also insisted that he was not a Fascist and would not become one, unless fascism were the only alternative to Marxism, a possibility which he regarded as unlikely.[17] Although Waugh's imperialism, his sense of racial superiority, and his conservatism led him to extreme rightist positions, we can conclude that he was never a convinced Fascist. To be sure, Waugh's persona, Gilbert Pinfold, is harassed by a sense of political guilt, so harassed, in fact, that in the midst of his hallucinations he is driven to make a truculent apologia to a fellow passenger on the *Caliban*: "I had every sympathy with Franco during the Civil War," bedeviled Pinfold declares, but, "I never had the smallest sympathy with Hitler." And though Pinfold admits that he once "had hopes of Mussolini," he asserts that he "was never connected with Mosley."

Nothing could be more hostile to Evelyn Waugh's political romanticism than fascism and nothing more distant from his social ideal than a totalitarian state. Buried in the midst of *Waugh in Abyssinia* is an episode which reveals, much more clearly than the foolish panegyric to the Italian army's civilizing impulses, the essence of Waugh's political sensibility and the conservative point of view from which he directs his satire. En route to the front lines, Waugh and a companion were entertained by an elderly district governor, Dedjasmach Matafara, a veteran of the first battle of Adowa. This gentlemanly patriarch greeted his English visitors with "great politeness and dignity" and, courteously helping them to choice tidbits from his own meal, entertained them with a curry and mugs of *tedj*. After ceremonial conversation,

Waugh departed, "slightly drunk," accompanied by soldiers whom the governor directed to protect the Englishmen on their way to Dessye. Of this experience, Waugh wrote:

> It had been more than a pleasant interlude; it had been a glimpse of the age-old traditional order that still survived, gracious and sturdy, out of sight beyond the brass bands and bunting; the topees and humane humbug of Tafari's regime; of an order doomed to destruction. Whatever the outcome of the present war: mandate or conquest or internationally promoted native reform—whatever resulted at Geneva or Rome or Addis Ababa, Dedjasmach Matafara and all he stood for was bound to disappear. But we were pleased to have seen it and touched hands across the centuries with the court of Prester John.

Waugh owes his allegiance to the passing order that his Abyssinian host symbolizes, and not to the totalitarian present. During the forties and fifties, his complaints about the confiscation of his earnings by taxation and about the machinations of bureaucracy often resembled the tired clichés of disgruntled Tories, but his real allegiance is to an ideal of the aristocratic life which exists only in his imagination. Waugh has stated that he has never voted in a Parliamentary election; and, in the portrait of himself drawn in *Gilbert Pinfold*, he describes his political stand as "an idiosyncratic toryism which was quite unrepresented in the political parties of his time."

Evelyn Waugh is apparently convinced that everything meaningful—the British Empire as a civilizing force, the English aristocracy, Western civilization, the English language itself—is threatened, near dissolution, or dying. Even the Roman Catholic church, he laments in the preface to *Sword of Honour*, has not been spared a "superficial revolution." The jungle is closing in again, Waugh believes; civilized man has been "leaving his post." A new dark age confronts us, and its standard-bearers, "drab, grey and brown," are the "Storm Troopers and the Partisans." The modern age is in arms, and Waugh wants none of it: the

Tory party or fascism no more than Labour or communism. Consequently, Waugh's "conservative" satires—*Black Mischief, Scoop, Scott-King's Modern Europe, Love Among the Ruins, Men at Arms, Officers and Gentlemen,* and *Unconditional Surrender*—either ridicule the political tendencies of the present or toll the bell for a passing order. "It is surely better," Waugh once wrote, in a sentence which explains his political attitude and the point of view from which the political satires are written, "to be imposed upon by a past which one has not seen than by a present of which one is oneself a part," and, he might have added, of which one thoroughly disapproves.[18]

CHAPTER XII

Darkest Africa, Dimming Europe, and the Dreary Future

BLACK MISCHIEF and *Scoop* are satires of empire, subtly different from such novels as E. M. Forster's *Passage to India* and George Orwell's *Burmese Days.* Though Waugh ridicules the practices of imperialism, he is not hostile to it, as a man of liberal impulse might be, for the injustice of its underlying assumptions. His African satires certainly do not exhibit the optimistic imperialism of Rudyard Kipling's time, and they mock both the doctrine of progress and the notions of sentimental reformers. They even disdain the qualified and sophisticated humanism we find in Forster and Orwell. Waugh's political satires are frankly conservative. For him there is an incorrigible savagery on this earth that cannot be redeemed by our notions of social improvement. In one uproarious scene of *Black Mischief,* His Britannic Majesty's Minister, Sir Samson Courtenay, a dithering fool of a man, appears at play, in his bath, with an India-rubber sea serpent; he signifies not that imperialism itself is idiotic but that an imperialism based on all that is most fatuous in "civilization" is. As Waugh sees it, savagery can be neither extirpated nor reformed; it can, at best, merely be contained.

Frederic Stopp, Waugh's Jungian analyst, finds in *Black Mischief* and *Scoop* the working out of the satirist's subconscious impulses and the manifestation of "fantasy," "vital urges," and "the unconscious springs of mythical action."[1] Nevertheless, the satire in the two novels has been consciously and deliberately directed at its objects. In both novels, chaos and disorder, provoked by modern political movements, are mastered and ordered; in *Black Mischief* the agency which brings order into chaos is a joint British-French protectorate over the African kingdom of Azania, and in *Scoop* it is the manipulation of force by an eccentric and cosmopolitan Englishman, who has purchased the mineral rights of Ishmaelia, an African republic.

The opening passage of *Black Mischief* conveys the tone and theme of the whole:

> *We, Seth, Emperor of Azania, Chief of the Chiefs of Sakuyu, Lord of Wanda and Tyrant of the Seas, Bachelor of the Arts of Oxford University, summoned by the wisdom of Almighty God and the unanimous voice of our people to the throne of our ancestors, do hereby proclaim* . . . Seth paused in his dictation and gazed out across the harbor where in the fresh breeze of early morning the last dhow was setting sail for the open seas. "Rats," he said; "stinking curs. They are all running away."

Throughout the novel, savage irony slashes into the mock-heroic posturing of Seth; his inflated pretensions are constantly deflated by the realities of barbarism. Though, as the novel opens, he is being deserted by all his supporters—one of whom decamps with the shabby crown—Seth is restored to authority when General Connolly defeats the rebellious forces of Seyid. Seth at once assumes that the victory has been won by his new armored tank, and he hymns the praises of the present. "Tipsy with words," he exults that he and the civilization he admires bring to his people "Light and Speed and Strength, Steel and Steam, Youth." Not even when General Connolly tells him that the battle was won by old weapons, "lies and the long spear"; that the "tin can," a furnace after a few hours in the Azanian sun, has been useful only as a punishment cell; and that Seth's father, Seyid, has been eaten by the Wanda, is the Emperor chastened.

When Seth discovers in Basil Seal "a man of culture, a modern man," the reign of "Progress" and "the New Age" are inaugurated in Azania. Seth spins crazily from "reform to reform," with little consideration of the means used to achieve the new age. The sincere but confused young man becomes "capricious and volatile"; ideas bubbling up within him bear "to the surface a confused sediment of phrase and theory, scraps of learning half understood and fantastically translated." Finally Seth comes a cropper: already having angered most of the powerful chiefs in his kingdom, he sets out to introduce birth control to his subjects. The Nestorian patriarch, whose orthodoxy is more certain than his virtue, immediately initiates a plot to restore the throne to the almost forgotten pretender. In the ensuing chaos, Seth is murdered.

Ironic leitmotifs that emerge from time to time indicate both the futility of Seth's dream of civilization and the impossibility of any real change in the kingdom. The motif of cannibalism, for example, initiated by the reference to Seyid's fate, is developed by subsequent descriptions of native banquets at which great, bloody slices of raw meat are devoured. The theme is further elaborated by the episode in which the army, issued boots, holds a feast to consume the whole lot; and it is culminated by the death of Prudence. Another such Firbankian motif is the Arab taxi. This rusty, derelict motor car blocks the main avenue into Matodi; a Sakuyu family has set up housekeeping in it. The taxi crops up again and again in the satire: either the resistance of the native family or the lethargy of Seth's workers prevents its removal. It remains after Seth's demise, and the English, we learn, have decided to rebuild the road around it.

The satirical irony of *Black Mischief* is thus entirely pessimistic—it suggests not only that Seth's reforms were foolish but also that the primitive African country is entirely impervious to civilization. Seth and all his associates are swept away; only Mr. Youkoumian, Waugh's transformation of that man of the world Mr. Bergebedgian, survives. He flourishes under the protectorate as he had throughout Seth's troubled reign. We learn that he has bought up what remains of Seth's railroad and does a thriving business supplying the English colony with tinned foods. He is an amoral and indestructible force, of the sort, as Waugh argued in *Remote People, Waugh in Abyssinia,* and *Robbery Under Law,* that alone determines the relations between nations.

Order of a kind has been instituted by the League of Nations' protectorate over Azania. In the English colony, identical bungalows have appeared; hierarchical and precise social distinctions have been instituted among the officials. As the novel closes, the mocking sound of Gilbert and Sullivan, played on a gramophone, wafts over the city:

> "Is it weakness of intellect, birdie?" I cried,
> "Or a rather tough worm in your little inside?"
> With a shake of his poor little head, he replied,
> "Oh, willow, tit-willow, tit-willow!"

Yet even this degree of ludicrous order has emerged only through force; what is happening in the English colony can have no bearing on the horrors that will continue to be perpetrated in the interior. The only possibility is that there will be, to use Mr. Youkoumian's phrase, no "bust-ups." The status quo can be maintained: the bars in Matodi can be closed at ten-thirty, and the colonials can try to prevent the jungle from creeping out to engulf them. It would be "weakness of intellect," *Black Mischief* implies, to believe that any further mastery may be gained over the forces of anarchy.

Waugh once explained why he journeyed to such countries as Ethiopia, British Guiana, and Brazil. "There is a fascination," he wrote, "in distant and barbarous places, and particularly in the borderlands of conflicting cultures and states of development, where ideas, uprooted from their traditions, become oddly changed in their transplantation."[2] One advantage of the African setting of *Black Mischief* and *Scoop* is that Waugh can reveal certain "modern" ideas jostling with primitive instincts and becoming grotesquely altered. As a result, he is able to satirize not only barbarism but also those contemporary "progressive" ideas he scorns.

Nothing in the general satire of modern progressivism in *Black Mischief* is more wicked and amusing than the treatment of Seth's attempt to introduce birth control among the natives. Although the majority of the clergy—excepting the Anglican Bishop, who resignedly explains that the English community is "already fully informed and equipped in the matter"—is hostile to the program, Seth is determined to carry it out. An Armenian artist, a friend of Mr. Youkoumian, naturally, elaborates on "a collection of highly inspiring Soviet posters" and produces the "highest triumph" of the new Ministry of Modernisation. His poster portrays two contrasting scenes:

On one side a native hut of hideous squalor, overrun with children of every age, suffering from every physical incapacity—crippled, deformed, spotted and insane; the father prematurely aged with paternity squatted by an empty cook-pot; through the door could be seen his wife, withered and bowed with child bearing, desperately hoeing at their inadequate crop. On the other side a bright parlor furnished with chairs and a table; the mother, young and beautiful, sat at her ease eating a huge slice of raw meat; her husband smoked a long Arab hubble-bubble (still a caste mark of leisure . . .), while a single healthy child sat between them reading a newspaper. Inset between the two pictures was a detailed drawing of some up-to-date contraceptive apparatus and the words in Sakuyu: WHICH HOME DO YOU CHOOSE?

An uproarious example of the satirical irony of inversion follows as Waugh describes native reaction to the poster:

See: on the right hand: there is a rich man: smoke pipe like big chief: but his wife she no good: sit eating meat: and rich man no good: he only one son.

See: on left hand: poor man: not much to eat: but his wife she very good, work hard in field: man he good too: eleven children: one very mad, very holy. And in the middle: Emperor's juju. Make you like that good man with eleven children.

The irony of *Black Mischief* is multiple; it is directed not only at the primitive mind but also at the follies of progressive thought, which, as Waugh regards it, so often does not take into account the intransigent irrationality of man.

In the African satires, Waugh sports with certain other "modern" ideas—humanitarianism and the free press—which he also manages to ridicule by projection against a primitive culture. Dame Mildred Porch and her colleague, Miss Tin, who, in *Black Mischief*, investigate Azania as members of a society for the prevention of cruelty to animals (and thus carry humanitarianism to an antihuman extreme), are based on two women described in *Remote People.* These latter ladies "were out for Vice"; planning a book on prostitution and the drug traffic, they were, according to Waugh, "too dense to find evidence of either."[3] When they appear as Dame Mildred and Miss Tin, their stupidity performs a useful service; they play the role of innocents in the satire. Witnessing the burlesque birth control pageant, these ladies admire the parade of schoolgirls and the floats on which pose local prostitutes. Observing the colorful banners, "WOMEN OF TO-MORROW DEMAND AN EMPTY CRADLE" and "THROUGH STERILITY TO CULTURE," Miss Tin says, "Very sensible and pretty."

The ideas of these ladies, who worry about "doggies" and ignore starving children, are strangely twisted when Viscount Boaz, somewhat confused about their cause, rises to praise them at a banquet. "It is to the great nations of the West and North," he concludes, "and especially to their worthy representatives that are with us to-night, that we look as our natural leaders on the road of progress. Ladies and gentlemen we must be Modern, we must be refined in our cruelty to animals." We need not share Waugh's political views to feel that this sort of satire makes its point truly. It is an effective antidote to foolish sentimentality and a rebuke to the hypocritical refinement of Europe's "modern" cruelties, cruelties with which Dame Mildred and Miss Tin might better concern themselves.

No less telling is Waugh's sharp thrust at the modern press in *Scoop*. Lord Cooper sends William Boot off to Ishmaelia with the *Beast*'s policy ringing in the fledgling's ears: the patriots are in the right and must win; in fact, the war must be over by the middle of July. However, ironically, when the gentlemen of the press encounter the wild improbabilities and fantastic confusions of life in Ishmaelia, they must necessarily invent even greater improbabilities to satisfy editorial policy and the cravings of the public. (It might be noted, incidentally, that George Orwell also distrusted the press.)

A less bitter satire than *Black Mischief*, *Scoop* is also more diffuse in structure and less incisive in its handling of the clash between political chaos and order. *Scoop* effects a curious transformation of the materials of *Waugh in Abyssinia* and of the Italian aggression against Haile Selassie's kingdom.

In both *Remote People* and *Waugh in Abyssinia,* Haile Selassie presented Waugh with a difficulty. The satirist was markedly hostile to this ruler; and yet the Emperor was not an easy object to ridicule, since he was not really a ludicrous figure and had already stamped upon the history of his time an image of discretion and dignity. Waugh's attempt to expose the "humbug" of Haile Selassie's regime–as in his description of the Emperor's visit to a hospital of war-wounded who were really venereal patients, deserters, and criminals–never does make Tafari himself look foolish. Waugh therefore pursued a second tactic in his treatment of Tafari: he indicated that the Emperor's reliance on the League was never sincere, that it merely cloaked his manipulation of the great powers and his deliberate provocation of Mussolini. As evidence, Waugh cited the negotiations into which Haile Selassie entered with a certain Mr. Rickett. To this agent of British-American interests, the Emperor, in an obviously desperate gamble to gain English and American protection, granted a concession of mineral rights. Though Waugh stated that the Emperor could not be reproached for this act, he described it in detail, evidently to substantiate his attitude that Haile Selassie was a shifty character who had been grossly sentimentalized by "liberals."

In treating the *Jeunesse d'Ethiopie,* the progressive organization of educated young men which Haile Selassie established to help modernize the kingdom, however, Waugh made no effort at all to be indirect. He obviously detested the "push and polish" of the group, its hostility to the clergy (an attitude which Waugh's own satire justifies), and its aims. If the *Jeunesse d'Ethiopie* "had succeeded," he insisted, "they would have created a country that was independent, powerful, uniform and utterly drab."[4]

The Rickett affair also provided Waugh with other elements which suffered a sea-change in *Scoop.* The day that the story of the concession broke in the press, Waugh found himself not at Addis Ababa but at Jijiga, where he and Patrick Balfour had just learned of the arrest of a rather seedy French count for espionage in the service of the Italians. As a result, Waugh's own scoop was completely ignored, and he received this importunate wire from his paper: "Badly left oil concession suggest you return Addis immediately."[5]

In Waugh's fictional spoof of the Italo-Ethiopian war, Abyssinia has been transformed into Ishmaelia. Of this country we learn that, "As there was no form of government common to the peoples . . . nor tie of language, history, habit or belief, they were called a Republic." No figure corresponding to Haile Selassie appears in the satire; instead we find that the government is in the hands of President Rathbone Jackson and the Jackson family, who remain shadowy figures. In short, Waugh has been unable to introduce the real Tafari, even greatly modified, into the satire. The *Jeunesse d'Ethiopie,* transformed into the Young Ishmaelites, does appear, however. It is controlled by Dr. Benito, who is in charge of foreign affairs and propaganda; he is a sinister figure. There is one other striking transformation of the actual events of the war: in *Scoop,* the conflict which is supposed to break out at any minute involves not foreign Fascists and native peoples but a civil antagonism between Fascists and Communists, who are receiving aid from the interested European powers.

The jumbled ideological consequences of this conflict are ridiculed when William Boot's editor attempts to describe the political alignments of Ishmaelia:

> You see they are all Negroes. And the Fascists won't be called Black because of their racial pride, so they are called White after the White Russians. And the Bolshevists *want* to be called Black because of *their* racial pride. So when you say Black you mean Red, and when you *mean* Red you say White, and when the party who call themselves Blacks say Traitors they mean what we call Blacks, but what we mean when we say Traitors I really couldn't tell you.

The levity of the parody in this passage certainly indicates no more respect for the absurdities of Fascist ideology than for those of Communist dogma. The villains of *Scoop* are, nevertheless, the Red Blacks. Waugh has pushed the progressivism of the *Jeunesse d'Ethiopie* far to the left, and the Young Ishmaelites, who have been "bought," have emerged as Communist plotters. At the climax of the novel, Dr. Benito, who has locked President Jackson in his room and begun negotiations with a Russian agent, declares Ishmaelia a Communist state. The Fascists, in the person of a German mineralogist, have receded far into the distance along with the President and his family. Only the British empire, in the person of William Boot, remains to challenge Benito.

Waugh's *ingénu* hero, supplied with the actual facts of the situation by Katchen and the English Vice Consul, gets the scoop his creator missed and sets out to accomplish a mission. He wants to protect the interests of "H. M. G." which "stands to lose a lot" if a soviet state is established; and he wants to "do down Benito," whom he has grown to detest. Waugh's tone, as he describes Boot's mission, is mock heroic, but his images are those of empire:

> Dimly at first, then in vivid detail, he foresaw a spectacular cinematographic consummation, when his country should rise chivalrously to arms: Bengal Lancers and kilted Highlanders invested the heights of Jacksonburg; he at their heads burst open the prison doors; with his own hands he grappled with Benito. . . . Love, patriotism, zeal for justice and personal spite flared within him as he sat at his typewriter and began his message.

If Boot's scoop catapults him to fame in England, it does not, however, trouble the new Communist state. So Boot appeals for a resolution to the conflict and for "a god from the machine." Immediately, the sound of an airplane is heard in the heavens, and, a moment later, a parachute bearing Mr. Baldwin floats to the roof of William's *pension*. The ubiquitous, ambidextrous, multilingual millionaire lands daintily on pointed, snakeskin toes, combs his purple hair, and takes the situation in hand. In this way Mr. Rickett has been transformed into a figure of grotesque satire. His fictional person, though, is not only more bizarre than his original but more successful. He explains to William the principles on which he operates: "*Might must find a way.* Not 'Force' remember; other nations use 'Force'; we Britons alone use 'Might.' Only one thing can set things right—sudden and extreme violence, or better still, the effective threat of it." Mr. Baldwin complains that his countrymen are now painfully tolerant of great losses by their capitalists and "sighs for the days of Pam or Dizzy." He has little difficulty, nonetheless, in effecting a counterrevolution on his own initiative. Exploiting the might of a drunken Swede who hates Russians, Mr. Baldwin leads a successful attack on the Residence. The climactic sequence unfolds "with the happy inconsequence of an early comedy film," as the Swede, in a parody of counterrevolution, drives the Young Ishmaelites to leap from the balcony of the Residence "onto the wooly pates below." Benito, we read, "was the last to go, proclaiming class war with his last audible breath." The delighted populace sets up a cry for President Jackson, Mr. Baldwin's friend. Free enterprise and imperialism carry the day.

Scoop is a lively and amusing work, and it is one of the early satires that *does* offer some positive alternatives to the conditions it rejects. But the alternatives are not particularly inspiring. Boot's flight to the nursery is pure escapism. The might exerted by Mr. Baldwin differs only in degree, and not in kind, from the force employed by Benito; and capitalist skulduggery and imperialism are scarcely moral alternatives to Communist machinations. Consequently, Waugh has to present even his "positives" through mock heroics and grotesquery. Nor does *Scoop* have the serious relevance to the realities of modern political life that *Black Mischief* has. (Recent events in the Congo seem to me to confirm Waugh's insights in *Black Mischief*.)

Waugh's satires, even at their most extravagant, generally do convince the reader that they reflect the realities of Waugh's time; but *Scoop*'s wild improbabilities are too distant from the real world to ring true. In transforming his experiences of the Ethiopian war into a satirical novel, Waugh seems to have lost contact with the issues of the conflict taking place in the thirties. If subconscious impulses have shaped the structure in any of Evelyn Waugh's novels, they may have done so in *Scoop*. For the action of this satire, with its transformation of the conflict into a clash between Communist duplicity and British might and its dependence on *deus ex machina*, is a perfect example of conservative wish-fulfillment.

Two grim, short political satires with none of *Scoop*'s ebullience or consolation—*Scott-King's Modern Europe* and *Love Among the Ruins*—followed the Second World War. The first of these recounts the visit of Scott-King, Classical Master at Granchester for twenty-one years, to a mythical totalitarian state called Neutralia. The second satire was in the tradition of *Brave New World* and *1984*; Waugh's inverted Utopia depicted a fully socialized England of the near future. Both works are bleakly pessimistic in outlook.

The form of *Scott-King's Modern Europe* resembles that of *Scoop*; the opening and conclusion of the novel, which place Scott-King at Granchester, frame the confusions and distractions of his journey to the tercentenary of Bellorius, Neutralia's late Latin poet, in the same way that the Boot Magna sections of *Scoop* frame the terrors of William Boot's journey to Ishmaelia. Waugh himself has made the most penetrating analysis of *Scott-King's Modern Europe*. Explaining to an interviewer that he was sure "there's a good thing hidden away in" the satire "somewhere" but that he had not "done it," Waugh said that if he were to do the book over he would try to suggest "more of the real horror" of such a journey. Burdened with "too much insignificant detail"[6] for so short a piece, as Waugh admitted, *Scott-King's Modern Europe* does not convey any of the real terrors of the contemporary totalitarian state. Waugh's subject is not, to be sure, Nazi Germany or Soviet Russia. A small "republic" which has managed to remain on the sidelines during the Second World War, Neutralia is, nevertheless, "a typical modern state, governed by a single party, acclaiming a dominant Marshal, supporting a vast ill-paid bureaucracy."

Waugh directs his satire at the absurd pretensions of Neutralia, which contrast with its seedy reality, and at the clumsy propagandistic motive of the bogus tercentenary. His Neutralia, reminiscent of Anthony Powell's Venusberg, is a mélange of baroque memorials and shabby, unfinished modern buildings. The Neutralian officials—Dr. Arturo Fe, who is in charge of the program, and Bogadin Antonic, a minor bureaucrat—are engaged in a desperate struggle for survival against inflation, low wages, and rivals. At the banquet honoring the visiting dignitaries, the servants stuff their pockets with food for their families. The real purpose of the celebration soon becomes obvious. Scott-King and his fellow guests are duped into attending a luncheon at party headquarters and visiting the memorial of a particularly vicious massacre; photographs of the compromised delegates are distributed to the press. The delegates fall out among themselves when they discover that they are being used for Neutralian propaganda; and only Scott-King, who has been accused of being a "Fascist beast," attends the unveiling of a memorial to his ideal, Bellorius, composer of a poem that had celebrated a rational Utopia in Latin hexameters. The statue, like the tercentenary celebration, is a travesty:

> The figure now so frankly brought to view had lain long years in a mason's yard. It had been commissioned in an age of free enterprise for the tomb of a commercial magnate whose estate, on his death, had proved to be illusory. It was not Bellorius; it was not even the fraudulent merchant prince; it was not even unambiguously male; it was scarcely human; it represented perhaps one of the virtues.

If Waugh was entitled to emphasize only the shabbiness, phoniness, and poverty of such totalitarian regimes as those of Spain and Yugoslavia (the countries that provided him with models for Neutralia) and to ignore their more vicious aspects, he ought, at the same time, to have softened the ending of *Scott-King's Modern Europe*. Nothing in the middle of the satire prepares for the ironic pessimism of the conclusion. To be sure, Scott-King has had to escape from Neutralia by the underground—not because he was in danger from the regime, but because his own consulate would not help him—and has consequently turned up stark naked in a camp for illicit immigrants in Palestine. But such satire is directed primarily at the difficulties of travel in modern Europe in the period following the Second World War and only secondarily at the evils of totalitarianism. Consequently,

Scott-King's abandonment of the rationalist idealism of Bellorius and his refusal, on returning to Granchester, to do anything "to fit a boy for the modern world" seem excessive reactions to his actual experiences. The defeatist tone of the conclusion of *Scott-King's Modern Europe* typifies Waugh's postwar satires. William Boot, at least, had been able to find security at Boot Magna Hall; Scott-King returns to Granchester to discover that there are fifteen fewer classical specialists for the coming term. And he is fully convinced, as the headmaster warns, that the time may come when there will be no more classical boys at all.

There are no classical boys in the England of *Love Among the Ruins.* Miles Plastic, the antihero of this satire, lives at a period perhaps two decades or so in the future; a product of a state orphanage, he has been scientifically reared to adjust to the modern world. The anti-Utopia in which Miles lives has definitely been influenced by other contemporary works in the genre. Waugh's "State be with you" echoes prayers and oaths in the name of Ford in Huxley's *Brave New World;* the golden beard of Waugh's heroine, consequence of an unsuccessful sterilization, suggests both the condition of the "freemartins" of *Brave New World* and the deformity of the heroine of *Ape and Essence.* Allusion to the prevalence of sexual promiscuity also associates Waugh's satire with Huxley's.

In its drabness, however, Waugh's totalitarian future resembles Orwell's *1984.* Scarcity, disorder, and grubbiness, rather than the glistening, antiseptic orderliness which Huxley described, characterize the England of the future as Waugh, following Orwell, has imagined it. As in Huxley's book and in Orwell's, the state is hostile to love, but it encourages promiscuity and frequent divorce. Certain details of *Love Among the Ruins* are similar to elements in the satirical poem "The Unknown Citizen" by W. H. Auden. The poem satirizes the tendency of the modern bureaucratic state to reduce human personality to a series of numbers and notations on file cards. The terms "Citizen" and "Modern Man," used to describe the subject of Auden's poem, are both applied to Miles Plastic, whose identity has also been reduced to a social psychologist's report. "In less than a minute," says the Deputy-Chief of the Ministry of Welfare, when Miles is released from corrective treatment, "you become a Citizen. This little pile of papers is *You*. When I stamp them, Miles the Problem ceases to exist and Mr. Plastic the Citizen is born."

These similarities to other satirical protests against the authoritarianism, dehumanization, and mechanization of life in the modern world are not defects in Waugh's novel. His short book is a much slighter anti-Utopia than Huxley's or Orwell's. *Love Among the Ruins* does not reveal such inventive fantasy as *Brave New World*, or the intellectual grasp of the nature of totalitarianism, accumulative power of sordid detail, and sense of evil of *1984*. Nevertheless, within its own limits, it is an effective variation on what has now become a traditional theme.

Little can be gained from judging such satires as *Brave New World*, *1984*, or *Love Among the Ruins* as prophecies of the condition of life in the future. The real point of these novels is that the brave new world is *now*; 1984 is 1944, 1954, or 1964; the ruins described in Waugh's short novel surround us. The satirical force of these works derives from the fact that the authors have carried to certain extremes of exaggeration tendencies which already undeniably exist. Huxley's soma, his feelies, his Malthusian drill are pointless if regarded as predictions; pertinent if regarded as parody of the abandoned materialism, mindless popular entertainments, and sexual indulgences of the present. Orwell's analysis of Newspeak, doublethink, and crimestop is, in fact, an analysis of the slave-mentality which sometimes dominates the modern world; the systematic destruction of the past which he describes is really, according to both Orwell and Waugh, what the newspapers have been doing for years, and the sport of heresy hunters throughout the world for many decades. Waugh's "ruins" are not in the remote future. The Dome of Security, whose eponymous dome, which had looked so well in the blueprints, failed even to show when the building was completed, is a travesty of the Dome of Discovery, a building in the best contemporary style erected for the 1951 Festival of Britain.[7] And Waugh's Department of Euthanasia is an exaggeration of the British public's interest in mercy killing.

Once again, the satirist launches an assault on a favorite subject: modern penology and that kind of social psychology which assumes that no man can "be held responsible for his own acts." The central attack in *Love Among the Ruins* is leveled at this denial of freedom of the will, a position which shocks Waugh as conservative and as Catholic. Mr. Sweat, an aged criminal who is receiving "corrective treatment" with Miles at the luxurious country seat, Mountjoy Castle, assails the modern attitude toward the criminal: "There's no understanding of crime these days like what there was. I remember when I was a nipper, the first time I came up before the beak, he spoke up straight: 'My lad,' he says, 'you are embarking upon a course of life that can only lead to disaster and degradation in this world and everlasting damnation in the next.' Now that's talking." But, alas, Mr. Sweat has fallen upon evil days; he has become, with Miles, an "antisocial phenomenon."

To achieve his satirical effect, as he sets out after the warped sentimentalism he regards as a feature of the welfare state, Waugh inverts all the traditional values. In the most painfully funny episode of the satire, Miles is brought before the court for having burned up an air force station and its occupants. "Arson, Wilful Damage, Manslaughter, Prejudicial Conduct, and Treason" have all been struck from the indictment, which has been reduced to the single charge of antisocial activity. The trial proceeds with the same illogical logic. "Widows, mothers, and orphans of the incinerated airmen" may resent the fact, but the hearing develops into "a concerted eulogy of the accused." The prosecution's old-fashioned attempt to emphasize the damages caused by the arson is futile; the judge insists that the jury expunge from its memory the sentimental details:

> "May be a detail to you," said a voice from the gallery. "He was a good husband to me."
>
> "Arrest that woman," said the judge.

When the jurymen bring in a verdict of guilty and recommend "mercy toward the various bereaved persons who from time to time in the course of the hearing had been committed for contempt," the judge reprimands them for impertinence and sends Miles off to the pleasures of Mountjoy Castle.

Sad epilogues to the history of Utopian literature, *Brave New World, 1984, Ape and Essence,* and *Love Among the Ruins* also make a striking commentary on contemporary history's impact on writers. When Aldous Huxley wrote *Brave New World* in 1932, he did offer some positive alternative to a mechanized and increasingly totalitarian world. Though his satire ended with the death of John the Savage, it indicated that something in human nature was impervious to total regimentation. Even after the Second World War, when Huxley wrote *Ape and Essence,* an infinitely depressing vision of life after the devastation of atomic warfare, he offered, as an alternative to the desolate, guilt-ridden, devil-worshiping society he described, the religious-communal society to which his hero and heroine escape. Orwell's *1984,* appearing a year later than *Ape and Essence,* suggested no alternative at all. Its antihero, Winston Smith, experiences a few elusive moments of happiness in his love affair with Julia; but the depressing conclusion of *1984* gives us a pair of lovers who, subjected to the diabolical torture of the Ministry of Love, have lost the one thing they believed could not be destroyed: their love for one another.

Waugh is no easier on us in *Love Among the Ruins.* As in *1984*, sexual love and some fragments of the past seem to grant his central characters a release from the drabness and tedium of society. When Miles meets Clara, the golden-bearded former ballet dancer, "hope" has appeared. In the cubicle of a Nissen hut, where Miles finds that Clara has preserved two eighteenth-century French paintings, a gilt clock, and a mirror framed in porcelain flowers, these two find a refuge from the hideous present. As in Orwell's work, however, the "state" will not countenance love. Because Clara is found to be with child, a more accomplished state surgeon than the first successfully completes the "Klugmann" that failed. He also manages to remove the skin of Clara's lower face and to substitute a synthetic rubber that takes grease-paint perfectly. Miles stares at the tight, slippery mask of salmon pink. He retches unobtrusively. Even Clara's unorthodoxy, her devotion to her art, for which she is willing to surrender everything, is corruptible by the state.

Miles has, to be sure, one other alternative—the pleasure of arson, which twice permits him to escape from being the "Modern Man." When the short satire ends, Miles is preparing to tour the country as the ministry's sole example of a successful corrective treatment—all others having died in the fire Miles set to destroy Mountjoy. In expectation of an early divorce, he is being married, as the Minister wishes, to Miss Flower, a "gruesome" young woman. Miles seems to have submitted completely to the scheme of things. But as his hand fidgets in his pocket during the ceremony at the Registry, it encounters his cigarette lighter. When Miles presses the catch, a flame rises, "gemlike, hymeneal, auspicious," and boding no good to Miss Flower.

This conclusion, mingling violence and the comic, is another example of Waugh's favorite shock effect. Its meaning, as a conclusion to the satire, is grim enough. Carried any further, the dehumanizing tendencies that the satirist observes in contemporary England may create a civilization in which rebellion itself can be only futile and destructive.* The full irony of the title of the work is borne home. In Browning's "Love Among the Ruins," the speaker, who surveys the ruins of a great city of the past, disdains the mortal glory which has passed away and turns to the love of the blonde girl who waits for him in the ruins; in Waugh's satire, no girl waits, and, as in *1984,* only the ruins remain.

* A recent novel in this tradition, *The Clockwork Orange* (London, 1962), by Anthony Burgess (who has certainly read his Waugh), actually develops this theme. It is not a cheerful book.

CHAPTER XIII

All Gentlemen Are Now Very Old

KINGSLEY AMIS, in attempting to explain new tendencies in the English novel of the 1950's, argued that pre-war satiric modes had been explicitly rejected. Nevertheless, when Amis described the attempt of certain recent English novelists to combine "the violent and the absurd, the grotesque and the romantic, the farcical and the horrific," he revealed that the influence of the early Huxley, Waugh, and Powell was still felt. Indeed, in *Men at Arms, Officers and Gentlemen,* and *Unconditional Surrender,* Evelyn Waugh revealed that he was as ready and able as ever to modulate effectively from one key to another.

Although since the time of *Brideshead* Waugh's manner has been modified by the attempt to adjust his satirical vision to a more conventional and realistic novel form, he has never, as Amis has suggested, abandoned satire.[1] The two principal satirical modes of the Guy Crouchback novels are burlesque and a particularly low-keyed ironic realism. The satirist's command of these two modes, exercised by means of a masterfully handled "counterpoint" technique, permits him successfully to achieve a satire with both positive and negative poles. In the three Guy Crouchback novels, Waugh does not permit waves of sentiment to dilute his satirical energy as he had in *Brideshead;* nor does his desire to express a positive value superior to the objects of his satire lead him into didacticism and satirical apology, as in *Helena*. In the Crouchback novels Evelyn Waugh successfully adjusts his conservative satirical vision to the conventions of the novel. These three novels are his most satisfying attempt to expose folly while creating meaningful positive values as well.

A number of strands in the complex web of these novels reveal how, despite their extraordinary pessimism, they affirm in a way that the early nihilistic works never could. Allusions to the great feast days, to the sacraments, and to the services of the Church are reminders, in all three, of a supernatural order that contrasts with the disintegrating forces of the war. These allusions are in no sense obtrusive; they form an inevitable part of the pattern of Guy Crouchback's existence. Guy's elderly father, who is often associated with these observances and rituals, embodies Waugh's social and religious ideals. This serene innocent has his comic side; he has, for example, acknowledged no English monarch since James II. Nevertheless, the chastity of his mind, the dignity of his bearing, and the essential decency of his spirit, all revealed to us from time to time in contrapuntal passages, function, as Waugh intended them, "to keep audible a steady undertone of the decencies and true purposes of life behind the chaos of events and fantastic characters."[2] Even the gentleness of Mr. Crouchback's "offstage" death, contrasting as it does with the violence of other deaths in *Unconditional Surrender*, serves to emphasize the importance of his role.

Then, too, Guy Crouchback himself, differing, as we have seen, from the antiheroes and victims of Waugh's earlier novels, helps to establish values. Inarticulate, frequently foolish, an easy dupe of illusion, limited by his social bias (though much less a snob than Charles Ryder), Guy Crouchback is, still, a man of honor and courage. In him, Catholicism and an aristocratic code of duty merge to offer a striking contrast to the vulgarity, cynicism, and amorality which are both cause and consequence of the war.

The symbolic figure of Roger of Waybrooke, a Christian knight of the Middle Ages, is constantly in Guy's consciousness. In Sir Roger, who appears throughout the trilogy as a standard of measurement, Waugh has again fused his conservative political commitment to an aristocratic tradition and his religious devotion to Roman Catholicism. Roger of Waybrooke, we learn at the opening of *Men at Arms,* was an English knight who set out for the Second Crusade. Sailing for Genoa, he was shipwrecked on the coast of Santa Dulcina. "There he enlisted under the local Count, who promised to take him to the Holy Land but led him first against a neighbor, on the walls of whose castle he fell at the moment of victory." As was Mr. Crouchback, Sir Roger, "a man with a great journey still all before him and a great vow unfulfilled," is delicately touched by Waugh's irony. Yet Sir Roger's quixotic idealism has had its own reward, for he is canonized in Santa Dulcina, where the people have taken him to their hearts. As Guy Crouchback sets off on his own quixotic crusade against the "Modern Age," an undertaking prompted by the Nazi-Soviet pact, he visits the tomb of Sir Roger to run his hand, as do the fishermen of Santa Dulcina, along the knight's sword. "Sir Roger, pray for me," he says, "and for our endangered kingdom."

An incident at Guy's club, soon after his return to England indicates that others do not approach the war with the same high purpose, devotion to moral cause, and disdain for the modern age in arms. It also reveals the central object of the conservative satire in both novels. When Guy indignantly criticizes the Russian invasion of Poland, for example, he finds no sympathy among the old soldiers who fill the club:

> "My dear fellow, we've quite enough on our hands as it is. We can't go to war with the whole world."

"Then why go to war at all? If all we want is prosperity, the hardest bargain Hitler made would be preferable to victory. If we are concerned with justice the Russians are as guilty as the Germans."

"Justice?" said the old soldiers. "Justice?"

Although the plot of *Men at Arms* deals with Guy's training and with his first experience of action in North Africa, a recurring leitmotif of ironic details carries the theme of national irresponsibility and dislocation of value that is to emerge in full force in *Officers and Gentlemen.* There are, for instance, Ian Kilbannock's air marshal ("the most awful shit"), for whom the war is an opportunity for gaining entrance to Bellamy's and for social climbing; Trimmer, another, though not deliberate, climber, "a slightly refined Cockney" type who is really more interested in trucking about the radio in a jazzy little dance than in becoming an officer in the Halberdiers; young Leonard, whose selfish wife nags him until, at the moment of the Brigade's departure for North Africa, he reluctantly applies for transfer, subsequently to die in a German bombing raid on London; and Halberdier Shanks, who applies for leave at the moment of the evacuation of Dunkirk so that he and his girl can perform the slow valse in a competition. Was this, Guy asks himself, the "spirit of Dunkirk"?

Officers and Gentlemen closes with England's bitter defeat on Crete and the development of the Russian alliance, which Guy regards as a betrayal of his crusade. In this book Waugh pushes to the fore the theme of the dissolution of moral, political, and social standards. Book One recounts the confused and disorderly period following Dunkirk and Guy's haphazard training with the commandos; Book Two is an account of the Cretan disaster, which Guy witnesses as an intelligence officer. The chaos that reigns on Crete is a more violent expression of the moral anarchy satirized in *Men at Arms* and in Book One of *Officers and Gentlemen.*

Mr. Crouchback's travails as a resident of the Cuthbert's

seaside hotel are only one ironic revelation of the decay of social values which the conservative Waugh regrets. When Mr. Crouchback's hosts enter into a conspiracy with the quartering officer to evict the aristocratic *ingénu,* he remains serenely unaware of their actual purpose. These shabby people—who would like to make a clean sweep of their guests, take people by the week, and so profit from the sufferings of those whose homes have been blitzed—simply cannot understand old Crouchback. When the old gentleman has been spared eviction by pure chance and patriotically surrenders his sitting room to another, Mr. Cuthbert suspects some duplicity: "He's a deep one and no mistake. I never understood him, not properly. Somehow his mind seems to work different than yours and mine." In effect, Mr. Crouchback—like the Dedjasmach Matafara of *Waugh in Abyssinia* and the Greek general who appears in Book Two, gracious amidst the chaos on Crete—is the survivor of an older and passing order. It may be said of Mr. Crouchback, as the cynical Corporal Ludovic says of General Miltiades, *"All gentlemen are now very old."*

In addition to this ironic realism in the account of Mr. Crouchback and the Cuthberts, burlesque is found throughout the novel, sustaining the pessimistic-conservative, satirical view of things. As the book opens, Ian Kilbannock's air marshal, frightened by an air raid, is discovered on all fours lurking under the pool table at Bellamy's. From this point on, a low burlesque metaphor of animalism mocks not only the inconsequence, confusion of purpose, and lack of principle marking the war effort, but also Guy's sense of mission as he sets out "on the second stage of his pilgrimage, which had begun at the tomb of Sir Roger." Gazing into a mirror after he has placed a gas mask over his face, still "full of hope and purpose," Guy sees a gross snout. An officer sulkily complaining to him of the short rations in the mess insists that, "We practically live . . . like wild beasts." When at last Guy sentimentally tracks his late friend Apthorpe's heir, Chatty Corner, to his "lair" on Mugg Island, where Guy is to be trained, he is greeted by a serving woman's "bark" and then by the shaggy, ape-like Chatty. Ivor Claire, who is to disillusion Guy, is first seen plucking the eyebrows of his Pekingese. Trimmer, who, after leaving the Halberdiers, assumed a false identity and re-enlisted, now emerges as McTavish, a kilted officer in a Scottish regiment. He is observed as he seeks amatory adventure in a Glasgow hotel; passing into the hotel's restaurant "with all the panache of a mongrel among the dust-bins, tail waving, ears cocked, nose a-quiver," Trimmer locates his prey when he meets Guy's former wife, Virginia, with whom he spends the week end. The triumph of sexual immorality reflects a social anarchy that would now seem to be complete.

This doggy burlesque reaches its apogee, however, in Book Two's counterpointing of the catastrophe on Crete with Trimmer's triumph on the home front. "Scottie," as Virginia's fashionable friends call him, continues in his "nosy and knowing" way to avoid actual combat. However, by ironic chance he is the only man available to lead Operation "Popgun," an aptly named expedition against a totally unimportant Channel island. The episode is a parody of warfare and an ironic inversion of what is happening on Crete. Purely by accident, Trimmer and his men, accompanied by a drunken Ian Kilbannock (now doing propaganda work), are landed on the Continent. When Trimmer discovers the error, he flees in terror to the waiting boat and, tripping over a railroad tie, receives a slight injury. His men blow up the railroad track. "We shall light such a candle by God's grace in England," Kilbannock proclaims in a drunken parody of Thomas Cranmer's words and in mock heroic apostrophe to Trimmer's exploit, "as I trust shall never be put out." In his drunkenness Kilbannock has spoken more truly than he knows, for Trimmer's exploit is taken up by the press, particularly (and appropriately) by the *Beast,* and he is puffed up into a national hero.

When it is discovered that Trimmer not only has "sex-appeal" but that his lower-class origins are a definite feature of his popularity, he is sent, as was that other modern man Miles Plastic, on a tour of English factories to boost morale and production. Since the "poor beast" is now in love with Virginia Troy, she is compelled, reluctantly, to accompany him.

Simultaneously, through the counterpoint, Waugh concentrates his satire on Major Hound, Guy's superior, a staff officer with no stomach for battle and no sense of honor, who is forced to take command of Hookforce when Tommy Blackhouse is injured. In the nether world of Crete, Hound, efficiency itself at headquarters, goes to pieces; his debasement typifies the entire Cretan episode and the loss of national honor. Soon Hound suggests that Guy call him by his nickname, "Fido." As his terror and confusion mount, he is more and more dehumanized and doggy. His "tail" is "right down"; he begins to scratch and snuffle. After a particularly harrowing German bombardment, he sights a culvert; Fido has found his "kennel." He creeps in, happily; "He found the curve of the drain comfortable . . . like a hunted fox, like an air marshal under a billiard table, he crouched in torpor." Finally, having deserted his command in the midst of the confused withdrawal, "Fido" is led by "delicious, doggy perceptions" to the scent of food, and to whatever unpleasant fate Corporal Ludovic, also a deserter, administers to him.

Officers and Gentlemen is not solely an aristocracy-worshiper's description of the collapse of values in the lower and middle classes during warfare, for Evelyn Waugh reveals, as burlesque turns into bitter irony, that even his aristocrats have failed him. Throughout the novel Guy has idealized Ivor Claire, whom he has regarded as the quintessential aristocrat, one of England's finest flowers, and the kind of man upon whom success in the war really depended. When Ivor is ordered to remain behind on Crete with the men who will face German prison camps, however, this fine flower of the aristocracy reasons that "honour" is "a thing that changes." He deserts his post, thinking of Freda, his Pekingese; and he has himself transferred to India, where he can stay out the war with his horses. As Guy recovers from the Cretan defeat and from the effects of his harrowing escape from the island in a small, open boat, he has to face another defeat: knowledge of Ivor's desertion. "After less than two years' pilgrimage in a Holy Land of illusion," Guy finds himself in a world where "gallant friends proved traitors and his country was led blundering into dishonour."

Yet this is not the most bitter irony of the novel. Before the final withdrawal from Crete, Guy finds the body of an English youth in a deserted village: "This soldier lay like an effigy on a tomb—like Sir Roger in his shadowy shrine at Santa Dulcina." The youth's identification disk indicates that he is a Roman Catholic; Guy, following regulations, carries it with him to Egypt. But Guy does not learn of the frivolous action which completes the betrayal of Sir Roger. When he turns over, for mailing to headquarters, an envelope containing the identification disk of the English soldier to Julia Stritch, the dazzling aristocrat of *Scoop,* she fears that Guy has given her evidence that might incriminate Ivor. Amoral to the core, Julia no longer appears as a delightful example of aristocratic indifference to convention. "Her eyes . . . one immense sea full of flying galleys," this pagan, this Cleopatra, drops the envelope into a wastepaper basket. In truth, the value Evelyn Waugh opposes to the chaos he burlesques or exposes through irony in *Officers and Gentlemen* cannot be identified with any class or group in contemporary England. The quixotic, aristocratic principle of devotion to honor and to God, which the symbolic figure of Sir Roger embodies, remains untarnished; but *Officers and Gentlemen* reveals not only the collapse of the class system but of those who Waugh, for many years, has believed should embody Sir Roger's ideals.

Unconditional Surrender, which appeared six years after *Officers and Gentlemen,* offers no relief from the social and historical pessimism of that book. It opens with a prologue that foreshortens the dreary experience of "two blank years," during which Guy is attached to a newly formed brigade of Halberdiers, only to be left behind to yet more dreary duties as a headquarters liaison officer when the Second Brigade leaves for action. "But it was not for this that he had dedicated himself on the sword of Roger of Waybrooke that hopeful morning four years back." In addition, Book One further intensifies Waugh's depiction of the betrayal of national honor; for the sword, which is "exposed for adoration" to the drab queues shuffling through Westminster Abbey, is a symbol, not of the nation's heroic past or present valor, but of the public's sentimental regard for its Russian ally. "It had been made at the King's command as a gift to 'the steel-hearted people of Stalingrad.' " The dandiacal Sir Ralph Brompton, an aging, homosexual diplomat and a Communist, emerges as a typical figure of the period. More fatuous than sinister, Sir Ralph has connections everywhere, and he moves behind the scenes throughout, advancing his causes (political and sexual) and influencing the course of events. Indeed, absurdly enough, it is Sir Ralph who eventually releases Guy from the tedium of liaison work and selects him for posting to Yugoslavia.

No doubt Waugh's hostility to the Russian alliance and his detestation of the Yugoslav Partisans produces a kind of historical astigmatism in him. In *Unconditional Surrender* his protagonist simply refuses to consider the historical and political necessities which led to the Anglo-American alliance with Russia and to the triumph of Tito and his Partisans. And yet, if the work constantly tends to overstate Communist influence on Anglo-American policy, I think the comic exaggeration of the role played by such figures as Sir Ralph and the ironic handling of the favor shown the Yugoslav Communists by Guy's superiors is no misrepresentation of the political and moral confusion prevalent during the closing months of the European war.

The novel reveals, at a deeper level of implication, Waugh's imaginative and moral grasp of the impulses released in the Second World War. Before the appearance of *Unconditional Surrender* and with the totally disenchanted conservatism of the first two volumes as evidence, it was doubtful whether in developing his announced theme—Guy's "realization that no good comes from public causes; only from private causes of the soul"—Evelyn Waugh would be able to suggest that the private cause of the soul need not isolate Crouchback from the rest of mankind, need not sever him from others. It was uncertain whether Waugh, having freed himself from romanticized devotion to a class, could attain some degree of that wide and generous sympathy which he had previously lacked. That Waugh does so without in the least compromising the profundity of his pessimism is a measure of the success of the final novel, and of the entire work.

In *Officers and Gentlemen* Corporal Ludovic, with his customary asperity, noted in his journal that Major Hound seemed "strangely lacking in the Death-Wish." The death wish dominates the final novel, just as a series of deaths punctuates the action. This is the force that moves in Virginia, when, after the birth of Trimmer's child, she cannot bear "its" presence; and it is the force that operates when she and Guy's Uncle Peregrine are killed by a doodle bomb. It is the title and pervasive mood of Ludovic's gaudy novel, a sick product of "disordered memory and imagination," composed by a Ludovic fleeing from memories of the reality of Crete. It moves Ben Ritchie-Hook to throw his life away in a fake Partisan attack during a mission to Yugoslavia. And it is the besetting sin to which Guy admits when he makes an act of confession. For in the last of these excellent novels Guy comes to understand not only that he was wrong in imagining that he might restore his own personal honor through acts of warfare, but that he, in common with all of Europe, has given himself not to life but to death.

Sensing that his commitment to a public cause has only frustrated the impulse behind it, Guy finally learns that charity is far more important than honor. When he decides to legitimatize Trimmer's child by remarrying Virginia, Kerstie Kilbannock attempts to dissuade him: " 'You poor bloody fool,' said Kerstie, anger and pity and something near love in her voice, 'you're being *chivalrous*—about *Virginia*. Can't you understand men aren't chivalrous anymore. . . ?' " Though he looks ridiculous, once again "playing the knight errant," Guy is no longer paying tribute to Sir Roger through violence. Understanding that he has never in his life performed a "single positively unselfish action," he sees his rescue of the distressed Virginia as a single small action, not sought after but thrust upon him, by which he may relieve the burden of human misery.

The third book of the novel contains the most moving passage Evelyn Waugh has written. Stationed at Bari, Guy is offered another chance "in a world of hate and waste" to perform "a single small act to redeem the times." Once again he does not seek the responsibility; instead, a group of Jewish "displaced persons"—refugees and survivors of concentration camps, victims first of Italian and German terrors and now of Partisan hostility—appeal to him for aid. Working through UNRRA, Guy attempts to evacuate them to Italy. Every effort he makes is thwarted, however, by the suspicion, stupidity, and anti-Semitism of the Partisans. Ironically, the "displaced persons" escape the Yugoslav camp where they have been interred only after the British mission has been removed from Bari. Guy sees them once again, in

Italy. They are as pathetic as ever, "back behind barbed wire in a stony valley near Lecce."

It is the least fortunate of these refugees, Madame Kanyi, a woman of superior intellect and perception, who enunciates the central insight to which the Crouchback novels lead. Madame Kanyi's husband runs the local power plant, and she is consequently a virtual prisoner of the Yugoslavs. After she leads the deputation of refugees who appeal to Guy for assistance, even her chance subsequent meetings with him are kept under surveillance by the hateful spy, Bakic. At a final, entirely innocent interview, when Guy carries a load of brushwood to her hut, Madame Kanyi sees the lurking form of the spy in the leafless shrubbery, and she asks: "Is there any place that is free from evil?" Her melancholy wisdom, the product of suffering and persecution, leads her then to suggest that it was not only the Nazis who wanted the war. The Communists wanted it too—to come to power; many of her own people wanted it—"to be revenged on the Germans, to hasten the creation of the national state." Indeed, she says, "there was a will to war, a death wish, everywhere. Even good men thought their private honor would be satisfied by war. They could assert their manhood by killing and being killed." And Guy responds in a moment of self-recognition: "God forgive me, . . . I was one of them."

Guy Crouchback's most shattering discovery of the ambiguity of human action and of the inevitability with which warfare corrupts comes later, when he learns from the odious and cowardly Gilpin (a Communist who has been attached to the British Mission by Sir Ralph Brompton) that his own last meeting with Madame Kanyi and even the stack of magazines he left behind for her have played a role in her terrible fate. She was, says Gilpin, "the mistress of the British Liaison Officer"; in her hut was found "a heap of American counter-revolutionary propaganda." The Kanyis, he boasts, were "tried by a People's Court. You may be sure justice was done." Tempted to strike a fellow officer, Guy drops his fist, overwhelmed by a sense of futility.*

Unconditional Surrender should not be read, as the two preceding volumes so easily can be, as a self-contained work. I do not mean to suggest that it is an imperfect work, for not only is the ordonnance of the books as satisfyingly proportioned and the prose as fine as in the earlier volumes, but its very quality of rounding off the first two novels is admirable. *Unconditional Surrender* completes the action of the trilogy most obviously in the way it traces Guy, his friends, and associates to the end of the war. We learn of the fates and lots of many individuals—the deaths of Mr. Crouchback, Uncle Peregrine, Virginia, and Ben Ritchie-Hook; the disappearance of Trimmer, the literary triumph of Ludovic; and finally the fruitful second marriage of Guy, who resides, as his father had hoped, in a small house on the family estate.

The book resolves the thematic conflict of the trilogy, for the happy ending reserved for Guy Crouchback is much more than a tidying up of plot and characters. It signifies Guy's return to life after disillusionment, descent into hell, and discovery of self. One of Waugh's funniest (and most profound) ironies is his counterpointing of the careers of Guy and Ludovic. For as Guy approaches a tragic awareness of his own limitations and reaches some understanding of the terrible ambiguity involved in any action, he emerges from the sterile isolation of his life as it was at the opening of *Men at Arms*. And, while Ludovic retreats ever deeper into fantasy (to escape from his Cretan memories and from his unfounded fear of Guy's knowledge), he absurdly assumes and grotesquely parodies Guy's earlier obsessions. He purchases a Pekingese and clownishly devotes himself to it, in a vain attempt to identify himself with Ivor Claire; in his overblown

* Apparently this episode of Madame Kanyi and the displaced persons has haunted Waugh's imagination, for he treated it once before in the short story "Compassion" (1949). As developed in *Unconditional Surrender*, it has even deeper resonances.

novel, he gives expression to the romanticism and aristocracy-worship that deluded Guy in the past. And finally, he purchases from Guy the Castello to which the latter had retreated when he isolated himself from others before the war.

As the enthusiastic reviewer for the *Times Literary Supplement* suggested, the Waugh of the Crouchback trilogy is very different from the author of the early novels; he has grown and extended the range not only of his expression but also of his sympathies.[3] Even in the most lighthearted scenes of the Crouchback novels we find overtones that simply did not exist in the more brittle early or middle works. For instance, when Guy's erring former wife dines with his prissy Uncle Peregrine, the following scene takes place:

> "Peregrine, have you never been to bed with a woman?"
>
> "Yes," said Uncle Peregrine smugly, "twice. It is not a thing I normally talk about."
>
> "Do tell."
>
> "Once when I was twenty and once when I was forty-five. I didn't particularly enjoy it."
>
> "Tell me about them."
>
> "It was the same woman."
>
> Virginia's spontaneous laughter had seldom been heard in recent years; it had once been one of her chief charms. She sat back in her chair and gave full, free tongue; clear, unrestrained, entirely joyous, without a shadow of ridicule, her mirth rang through the quiet little restaurant. Sympathetic and envious faces turned towards her. She stretched across the table cloth and caught his hand, held it convulsively, unable to speak, laughed until she was breathless and mute, still gripping his bony fingers. And Uncle Peregrine smirked. He had never before struck success. . . . He did not now quite know what it was that had won this prize, but he was highly gratified.
>
> "Oh, Peregrine," said Virginia at last with radiant sincerity, "I love you."

Virginia belongs, of course, in the line of Margot Maltravers and Brenda Last; but she has a genuineness and warmth never glimpsed in her predecessors. Waugh can now go beneath the impudence and the irresponsible charm of the type to discern Virginia's pathos, trapped as she is and beyond her youth. In a partly self-spoofing passage, he allows the pretentious editor Everard Spruce to relate the dead Virginia to a literary tradition: "Virginia Troy was the last of twenty years' succession of heroines. . . . The ghosts of romance who walked between the two wars." Her original, Spruce correctly senses, was Aldous Huxley's Mrs. Viveash; Michael Arlen's Iris Storm and Ernest Hemingway's Brett, a "coarsened" image, were her sisters. Virginia, Spruce announces in his extravagant rhetoric, "was the last of them–the exquisite, the doomed and the damning, with expiring voices–a whole generation younger. We shall never see any one like her again in literature or in life." Much as I admire the outrageous effects of *Vile Bodies* and *Black Mischief* and the brilliant, uncommitted irony of *A Handful of Dust,* I cannot regret that Evelyn Waugh came to a stage in his career when he could not only see Virginia, quite engagingly, in the perspective of literary history but also, without sentimentalism, make us feel her mortality.

Evelyn Waugh has not, indeed, been content to repeat himself.* Nor has he been willing for the Crouchback novels to be regarded as "separate and independent" works. In his preface to *Sword of Honour,* Waugh implies that the appearance of the novels "at intervals throughout a decade" may have tended to obscure their essential unity of conception, and he asserts that he has always intended his account of Guy Crouchback's experiences in the war "to be read as a single story." To that end, when he prepared his "recension" of the three works, he effaced the original structural divisions and divided the work into eleven chapters. He also excised a few passages and some minor details. (Regrettably, readers

* The thinness of the recent short story, "Basil Seal Rides Again," which Waugh describes in the dedication to the handsome limited edition as a "senile attempt to recapture the manner of my youth," reveals that he should not, indeed, try to return to that manner.

of the recension will find no reference to either Captain Truslove or General Miltiades.) The recension is, however, substantially the same as the original volumes; and some who feel that it was possible to read *Men at Arms* and *Officers and Gentlemen,* in particular, as autonomous works may be conscious of the original structural rhythms of the three volumes in the recension. Yet if Waugh, in his preface, seems to ignore the underlying tripartite structure of *Sword of Honour,* he has every right to insist that we see the wholeness of his work.

The imaginative unity of this major work of Waugh's later career is fundamental. The "Garibaldi" restaurant episode in *Men at Arms* and the mad Scottish Nationalist episode in *Officers and Gentlemen,* seemingly unrelated but actually linked, are but one token of Waugh's command of his material. In the first of these episodes, a restaurant proprietor who is also a part-time spy overhears Guy's conversation, absurdly misunderstands, and sends a confused report to his superiors. In the second, the lunatic grandniece of the laird of the Isle of Mugg deposits bundles of pro-German propaganda in an automobile Guy has used. Oddly distorted versions of both events find their way, eventually, to a top-secret file, establishing a record of pro-Fascist activity on the part of Captain Crouchback.

In themselves the incidents are crazily amusing, and they help to build up Waugh's picture of the sheer futility of much of the war effort. But they are also part of Waugh's total irony, for in *Unconditional Surrender,* despite the secret file, Guy is selected as a respectable front man in the Yugoslav mission that Sir Ralph Brompton has packed with Communists. And one of these Communists has the effrontery to report to Guy another false rumor, circulated by the Yugoslavs, that Madame Kanyi was a counter-revolutionary and the mistress of a British liaison officer!

Whether Waugh's narrative of Guy Crouchback's pilgrimage is read as a trilogy of closely related volumes or, in the omnibus edition, "as one story," there is no denying its artistic unity. The distancing critical power of time has established *A Handful of Dust,* I believe, as one of the most distinguished novels of its time. The very least that can be said of *Sword of Honour* is that it reveals an intense satiric vision of the social and moral consequences of the Second World War, that it constitutes the triumph of Evelyn Waugh's later manner, and that it represents a mature artist's highly individual commitment to life. The very qualification Waugh imposes on that commitment, his sense of the awful ambiguity of even the best of man's actions, serves to intensify it. Evelyn Waugh has made no surrender, unconditional *or* conditional, to the modern age. But when Guy Crouchback accepted Trimmer's child as his own and went to the aid of the displaced persons, his creator, undiminished in satiric power, revealed that pity too was within his range.

Notes

PREFACE

1. Evelyn Waugh, "Come Inside," *The Road to Damascus,* ed. John A. O'Brien (Garden City, N.Y., 1949), p. 20.

2. Evelyn Waugh, *When the Going Was Good* (London, 1946), p. 9.

3. *Ibid.,* pp. 9-10.

4. Eric Linklater, "Evelyn Waugh," *The Art of Adventure* (London, 1948), pp. 47-48.

5. *Ibid.,* p. 48.

6. Harvey Breit, "Evelyn Waugh," *The Writer Observed* (Cleveland, Ohio, 1956), p. 44.

7. J. B. Priestley, "What Was Wrong With Pinfold?" *New Statesman and Nation* (Aug. 31, 1957), p. 244.

8. Northrop Frye, "The Nature of Satire," *University of Toronto Quarterly,* XIV (October, 1944), 75.

9. *Satire Newsletter* (Fall, 1964).

CHAPTER I

1. G. S. Fraser, *The Modern Writer and His World* (London, 1955), p. 99.

2. Evelyn Waugh, "Ronald Firbank," *Life and Letters,* II (March, 1929), 191.

3. *Ibid.,* pp. 194-96. See also Jocelyn Brooke, *Ronald Firbank* (New York, 1951), p. 17.

4. Waugh, "Ronald Firbank," pp. 195-96.

CHAPTER II

1. Evelyn Waugh, "Fan-fare," *Life* (April 8, 1946), p. 60.
2. Stephen Spender, *The Creative Element: A Study of Vision, Despair and Orthodoxy* (New York, 1954), p. 163.
3. Eric Linklater, "Evelyn Waugh," *The Art of Adventure* (London, 1948), p. 47.
4. Evelyn Waugh, "The War and the Younger Generation," *Spectator* (April 13, 1929), p. 571.
5. Evelyn Waugh, "Death in Hollywood," *Life* (Sept. 29, 1947), pp. 73, 83, 84.

CHAPTER III

1. Eric Linklater, "Evelyn Waugh," *The Art of Adventure* (London, 1948), pp. 55-56.

CHAPTER IV

1. Nigel Dennis, "Evelyn Waugh: The Pillar of Anchorage House," *Partisan Review,* X (July-August, 1943), 353-54.
2. Donat O'Donnell (Conor Cruise O'Brien), *Maria Cross: Imaginative Patterns in a Group of Modern Catholic Writers* (New York, 1952), p. 121.
3. D. S. Savage, "The Innocence of Evelyn Waugh," *Focus Four,* ed. B. Rajan (London, 1947), p. 35.
4. A. A. DeVitis, *Roman Holiday: The Catholic Novels of Evelyn Waugh* (New York, 1956), p. 69.

CHAPTER V

1. Sean O'Faolain, *The Vanishing Hero* (London, 1956), pp. 16, 17.
2. Nigel Dennis, "Waugh: Pillar of Anchorage House," *Partisan Review,* X (July-August, 1943), 360.

CHAPTER VI

1. Evelyn Waugh, "Fan-fare," *Life* (April 8, 1946), p. 60.
2. Frederic J. Stopp, *Evelyn Waugh: Portrait of an Artist* (London, 1958), pp. 190-95.
3. Sean O'Faolain, *The Vanishing Hero* (London, 1956), p. 52.
4. Waugh, "Fan-fare," p. 56.
5. David Worcester, *The Art of Satire* (Cambridge, Mass., 1950), p. 120.
6. Nigel Dennis, "Waugh: Pillar of Anchorage House," *Partisan Review,* X (July-August, 1943), 350.
7. *Ibid.*

CHAPTER VII

1. Albert Camus, *The Rebel* (New York, 1956), pp. 10, 14-16.
2. Louis O. Coxe, "The Protracted Sneer," *New Republic* (Nov. 8, 1954), pp. 20-21.
3. Camus, *The Rebel,* p. 266.
4. Malcolm Bradbury, *Evelyn Waugh* (Edinburgh and London, 1964), p. 55. On the other hand, a French critic asserts, without qualification, that Waugh "est avant tout un satiriste et même un moraliste." See F. Lapicque, "La Satire Dans L'Oevre D'Evelyn Waugh," *Etudes Anglaises,* X (Juillet-Septembre, 1957), 193-215.
5. V. S. Pritchett, "Cleverest English Novelist Alive," *New Statesman and Nation* (May 7, 1949), p. 473.
6. Edmund Wilson, "Never Apologize, Never Explain," *Classics and Commercials* (New York, 1950), p. 146.
7. Evelyn Waugh, "Fan-fare," *Life* (April 8, 1946), p. 58.
8. Wilson, "Never Apologize, Never Explain," p. 143.
9. Stephen Spender, *The Creative Element: A Study of Vision, Despair and Orthodoxy Among Some Modern Writers* (New York, 1954), pp. 167-68.
10. David Worcester, *The Art of Satire* (Cambridge, Mass., 1950), p. 139.
11. Alan Reynolds Thompson, *The Dry Mock* (Berkeley, Calif., 1948), p. 5.

CHAPTER VIII

1. George Bernard Shaw, "The Quintessence of Ibsenism," *Selected Prose of Bernard Shaw,* ed. Diarmuid Russell (New York, 1952), p. 554n.

2. *Ibid.,* p. 550.

3. Calvert Alexander, *The Catholic Literary Revival* (Milwaukee, Wis., 1935), pp. 131-32.

4. R. A. Scott-James, *Fifty Years of English Literature* (London, 1956), p. 51.

5. Evelyn Waugh, "The Jesuit Who Was Thursday," *Commonweal* (March 21, 1947), p. 561.

6. Kathleen Nott, *The Emperor's Clothes* (Bloomington, Ind., 1958), p. 43.

7. Graham Greene, *Journey Without Maps* (London, 1953), p. 10.

8. Quoted in Philip Temple, "Some Sidelights on Evelyn Waugh," *America* (April 27, 1946), p. 75.

9. Karl Adam, *The Spirit of Catholicism* (New York, 1954), pp. 6-7.

10. Graham Greene, *The Lawless Roads* (London, 1955), pp. 51, 234.

11. Evelyn Waugh, "Come Inside," *The Road to Damascus,* ed. John A. O'Brien (Garden City, N.Y., 1949), p. 20.

12. *Ibid.,* pp. 18, 20.

13. Maurice Evans, *G. K. Chesterton* (Cambridge, Eng., 1939), p. 32.

14. Evelyn Waugh, "The American Epoch in the Catholic Church," *Life* (Sept. 19, 1949), p. 135.

15. Quoted in Temple, "Some Sidelights on Evelyn Waugh," p. 76.

16. Waugh, "Come Inside," p. 20.

17. Temple, "Some Sidelights on Evelyn Waugh," p. 76.

18. Evelyn Waugh, *Robbery Under Law* (London, 1939), p. 10.

19. Evelyn Waugh, "Felix Culpa?" *Commonweal* (July 16, 1948), p. 324.

20. Evelyn Waugh, "Heart's Own Reasons," *Commonweal* (Aug. 17, 1951), p. 458.

21. Evelyn Waugh, *Remote People* (London, 1934), pp. 88-89.

CHAPTER IX

1. Quoted in Donat O'Donnell (Conor Cruise O'Brien), *Maria Cross: Imaginative Patterns in a Group of Modern Catholic Writers* (New York, 1952), p. 119.
2. Edmund Wilson, "The Splendors and Miseries of Evelyn Waugh," *Classics and Commercials* (New York, 1950), pp. 298, 299.
3. Quoted in A. A. DeVitis, *Roman Holiday: The Catholic Novels of Evelyn Waugh* (New York, 1956), p. 41.
4. Sean O'Faolain, *The Vanishing Hero* (London, 1956), pp. 64-66.
5. DeVitis, *Roman Holiday*, p. 53.
6. Christopher Hollis, *Evelyn Waugh* (London, 1954), p. 20.
7. Linklater, "Evelyn Waugh," *The Art of Adventure* (London, 1948), p. 52.
8. Evelyn Waugh, "Heart's Own Reasons," *Commonweal* (March 21, 1947), p. 458.
9. Charles J. Rolo, "Evelyn Waugh: The Best and the Worst," *Atlantic Monthly*, CXCIV (October, 1954), 84.
10. O'Faolain, *The Vanishing Hero*, pp. 64, 65.
11. O'Donnell, *Maria Cross*, pp. 175-76.

CHAPTER X

1. Frederic J. Stopp, *Evelyn Waugh: Portrait of an Artist* (London, 1958), p. 205; Harvey Breit, "W. Somerset Maugham and Evelyn Waugh," *The Writer Observed* (Cleveland, Ohio, 1956), p. 149; Aubrey Menen, "The Baroque and Mr. Waugh," *The Month*, V (April, 1951), 237.
2. Jacob Burckhardt, *The Age of Constantine the Great* (New York, 1949), pp. 339-40.
3. Evelyn Waugh, "St. Helena Empress," *The Holy Places* (London, 1953), p. 11.
4. Evelyn Waugh, "Fan-fare," *Life* (April 8, 1946), p. 56.

CHAPTER XI

1. Evelyn Waugh, *Labels* (London, 1930), p. 20.

2. Aldous Huxley, "Accidie," *On the Margin* (London, 1923), p. 25.

3. Kathleen Nott, *The Emperor's Clothes* (Bloomington, Ind., 1958), pp. 125-39.

4. Harold H. Watts, *Ezra Pound and the Cantos* (London, 1951), p. 10; Geoffrey Wagner, *Wyndham Lewis: A Portrait of the Artist as Enemy* (London, 1957), pp. 80-86; Wyndham Lewis, *Snooty Baronet* (London, 1932), p. 182; Roy Campbell, *Flowering Rifle* (London, 1939), p. 51.

5. Waugh, *Labels,* pp. 40, 110; see also, Evelyn Waugh, *Rossetti* (London, 1928), p. 223; Wagner, *Wyndham Lewis,* pp. 48, 61; Evelyn Waugh, *Waugh in Abyssinia* (London, 1936), pp. 34, 215; Evelyn Waugh, "Through European Eyes," *London Mercury,* XXXVI (June, 1937), 147; Waugh, "The War and the Younger Generation," *Spectator* (April 13, 1929), p. 571; Campbell, *Flowering Rifle,* p. 8; Rose Macaulay, "Evelyn Waugh," *Writers of Today,* ed. Denys Val Baker (London, 1948), p. 146; Donat O'Donnell, *Maria Cross: Imaginative Patterns in a Group of Modern Catholic Writers* (New York, 1952), p. 240.

6. Albert Camus, *The Rebel* (New York, 1956), p. 180.

7. Frederic J. Stopp, *Evelyn Waugh: Portrait of an Artist* (London, 1958), p. 22.

8. Waugh, *Labels,* p. 57.

9. Evelyn Waugh, *Remote People* (London, 1934), pp. 68, 99, 111.

10. Waugh, *Labels,* p. 94; Waugh, *Remote People,* pp. 36, 138, 175, 176, 193; Evelyn Waugh, *Robbery Under Law* (London, 1939), pp. vii-viii.

11. Waugh, *Remote People,* pp. 20, 21, 29, 33, 45-48.

12. *Ibid.,* pp. 153, 183.

13. *Ibid.,* pp. 180-81, 191.

14. Waugh, *Waugh in Abyssinia,* p. 35.

15. *Ibid.,* pp. 40, 41, 129, 132, 253.

16. *Ibid.,* p. 253.

17. Evelyn Waugh, "Fascist," *New Statesman* (March 5, 1930), p. 365; Evelyn Waugh, in *Authors Take Sides,* an unpaged pamphlet compiled by Oakley Johnson (London, 1938).

18. Waugh, *Waugh in Abyssinia,* p. 202; Waugh, "Fan-fare," *Life* (April 8, 1946), pp. 53, 60; Evelyn Waugh, *The Holy Places* (London, 1953), p. 9; Stopp, *Evelyn Waugh,* p. 45; Evelyn Waugh, *When the Going Was Good* (London, 1946), p. 10; Evelyn Waugh, "Belloc Anadyoneme," *Spectator* (Aug. 26, 1955), p. 283; Waugh, *Labels,* p. 19.

CHAPTER XII

1. Frederic J. Stopp, *Evelyn Waugh: Portrait of an Artist* (London, 1958), pp. 80-86.

2. Evelyn Waugh, *When the Going Was Good* (London, 1946), p. 197.

3. Evelyn Waugh, *Remote People* (London, 1934), p. 44.

4. Evelyn Waugh, *Waugh in Abyssinia* (London, 1936), p. 67.

5. *Ibid.,* p. 109.

6. Harvey Breit, "Evelyn Waugh," *The Writer Observed* (Cleveland, Ohio, 1956), pp. 43-44.

7. Stopp, *Evelyn Waugh,* p. 46.

CHAPTER XIII

1. Kingsley Amis, "Laughter's to Be Taken Seriously," *New York Times Book Review* (July 7, 1957), p. 1.

2. Quoted in Frederic J. Stopp, *Evelyn Waugh: Portrait of an Artist* (London, 1958), p. 168.

3. "The New Waugh," London *Times Literary Supplement* (Oct. 27, 1961), p. 770.

Bibliography

I. PRIMARY SOURCES

Auden, Wystan Hugh. *The Collected Poetry of W. H. Auden.* New York: Random House, 1945.

Campbell, Roy. *Flowering Rifle.* London: Longmans, Green & Co., 1939.

Douglas, Norman. *South Wind.* New York: Modern Library, 1925.

Firbank, Ronald. *Five Novels.* Norfolk, Conn.: New Directions, n. d.

———. *Three Novels.* Norfolk, Conn.: New Directions, n. d.

Greene, Graham. *England Made Me.* Garden City, N.Y.: Doubleday & Co., 1935.

———. *Journey Without Maps.* London: William Heinemann Ltd., 1953.

———. *The Lawless Roads.* London: William Heinemann Ltd., 1955.

Huxley, Aldous. *Antic Hay.* New York: Modern Library, 1923.

———. *Brave New World.* New York: Harper & Brothers, 1950.

———. *Crome Yellow.* New York: Harper & Brothers, 1922.

———. *On the Margin.* London: Chatto & Windus, 1923.

Johnson, Oakley (compiler). *Authors Take Sides on the Spanish Civil War.* London: Left Review, 1938.

Lewis, Wyndham. *Satire and Fiction.* London: The Arthur Press, n. d.

———. *Snooty Baronet.* London: Cassell & Co., Ltd., 1932.

Orwell, George. *1984*. New York: Harcourt, Brace & Co., 1949.

Shaw, George Bernard. "The Quintessence of Ibsenism," *The Selected Prose of Bernard Shaw,* ed. Diarmuid Russell. New York: Dodd, Mead & Co., 1952.

Waugh, Evelyn. "American Epoch in the Catholic Church," *Life* (Sept. 19, 1949), pp. 134-55.

_______. "Basil Seal Rides Again: Or the Rake's Regress." London: Chapman & Hall, 1963.

_______. "Belloc Anadyomene," *Spectator* (Aug. 26, 1955), p. 283.

_______. *Black Mischief*. Boston: Little, Brown & Co., 1946.

_______. *Brideshead Revisited*. Boston: Little, Brown & Co., 1945.

_______. *Brideshead Revisited*. Revised ed. London: Chapman & Hall, 1960.

_______. "Come Inside," *The Road to Damascus,* ed. John A. O'Brien. Garden City, N.Y.: Doubleday & Co., 1949, pp. 17-20.

_______. "Death in Hollywood," *Life* (Sept. 29, 1947), pp. 73-84.

_______. *Decline and Fall*. Boston: Little, Brown & Co., 1949.

_______. *Edmund Campion*. London: Hollis & Carter, 1952.

_______. "Fan-fare," *Life* (April 8, 1946), pp. 53-60.

_______. "Fascist," *New Statesman* (March 5, 1938), p. 365.

_______. "Felix Culpa?" *Commonweal* (July 16, 1948), pp. 322-25.

_______. *A Handful of Dust*. Boston: Little, Brown & Co., 1952.

_______. "Heart's Own Reasons," *Commonweal* (Aug. 17, 1951), pp. 458-59.

_______. *Helena*. London: Chapman & Hall, 1950.

_______. *The Holy Places*. London: The Queen Anne Press, 1953.

_______. "The Jesuit Who Was Thursday," *Commonweal* (March 21, 1947), pp. 558-61.

_______. *Labels*. London: Duckworth, 1930.

_______. *A Little Learning: The First Volume of An Autobiography*. London: Chapman & Hall, 1964.

_______. *The Loved One*. London: Chapman & Hall, 1948.

_______. *Men at Arms*. London: Chapman & Hall, 1952.

_______. *Mr. Loveday's Little Outing and Other Sad Stories*. Boston: Little, Brown & Co., 1936.

_______. *Monsignor Ronald Knox.* Boston: Little, Brown & Co., 1959.

_______. *Ninety-Two Days: The Account of a Tropical Journey Through British Guiana and a Part of Brazil.* New York: Farrar & Rinehart, 1934.

_______. *Officers and Gentlemen.* London: Chapman & Hall, 1955.

_______. *The Ordeal of Gilbert Pinfold.* London: Chapman & Hall, 1957.

_______. *Put Out More Flags.* Boston: Little, Brown & Co., 1955.

_______. *Remote People.* London: Duckworth's Georgian Library, 1934.

_______. *Robbery Under Law: The Mexican Object-Lesson.* London: Chapman & Hall, 1939.

_______. "Ronald Firbank," *Life and Letters,* II (March, 1929), 191-96.

_______. *Rossetti: His Life and Works.* London: Duckworth, 1930.

_______. *Scoop.* Boston: Little, Brown & Co., 1949.

_______. *Scott-King's Modern Europe.* London: Chapman & Hall, 1950.

_______. *Sword of Honour.* London: Chapman & Hall, 1965.

_______. *Tactical Exercise.* Boston: Little, Brown & Co., 1954.

_______. "Through European Eyes," *London Mercury,* XXXVI (June, 1937), 147-50.

_______. *Tourist in Africa.* Boston: Little, Brown & Co., 1960.

_______. *Unconditional Surrender.* London: Chapman & Hall, 1961.

_______. *Vile Bodies.* Boston: Little, Brown & Co., 1955.

_______. "The War and the Younger Generation," *Spectator* (April 13, 1929), pp. 570-71.

_______. *Waugh in Abyssinia.* London: Longmans, Green & Co., 1936.

_______. *When the Going Was Good.* London: Duckworth, 1946.

II. SECONDARY SOURCES

Acton, Harold. *The Memoirs of an Aesthete.* London: Methuen & Co. Ltd., 1948.

Adam, Karl. *The Spirit of Catholicism.* Garden City, N.Y.: Image Books, 1954.

Alexander, Calvert. *The Catholic Literary Revival.* Milwaukee, Wis.: The Bruce Publishing Company, 1935.

Amis, Kingsley. "Laughter's to Be Taken Seriously," *New York Times Book Review* (July 7, 1957), pp. 1, 13.

Atkins, John. *Aldous Huxley.* London: John Calder, 1956.

Bradbury, Malcolm. *Evelyn Waugh.* (Writers and Critics.) Edinburgh and London: Oliver & Boyd, 1964.

Breit, Harvey. *The Writer Observed.* Cleveland, Ohio: World Publishing Company, 1956.

Burckhardt, Jacob. *The Age of Constantine the Great.* New York: Pantheon Books, 1949.

Camus, Albert. *The Rebel.* New York: Vintage Books, 1956.

Coxe, Louis O. "The Protracted Sneer," *New Republic* (Nov. 8, 1954), pp. 20-21.

Dennis, Nigel. "Evelyn Waugh: The Pillar of Anchorage House," *Partisan Review,* X (July-August, 1943), 350-61.

DeVitis, A. A. *Roman Holiday: The Catholic Novels of Evelyn Waugh.* New York: Bookman Associates, 1956.

Fraser, G. S. *The Modern Writer and His World.* London: Andre Deutsche, 1955.

Frye, Northrop. *Anatomy of Criticism.* Princeton, N.J.: Princeton University Press, 1957.

______. "The Nature of Satire," *University of Toronto Quarterly,* XIV (October, 1944), 75-89.

Hazlitt, William. "On Wit and Humour," *The Miscellaneous Works of William Hazlitt.* Boston: Estes & Laureat, n.d., Vol. III, pp. 1-31.

Hollis, Christopher. *Evelyn Waugh.* (Writers and Their Work, No. 46.) London: Longmans, Green & Co., 1954.

Linklater, Eric. "Evelyn Waugh," *The Art of Adventure.* London: The Macmillan Company, 1948, pp. 44-58.

Macaulay, Rose. "Evelyn Waugh," *Writers of Today*. 2nd series, ed. Denys Val Baker. London: Sidgwick & Jackson Ltd., 1948, pp. 135-51.

Menen, Aubrey. "The Baroque and Mr. Waugh," *The Month,* V (April, 1951), 226-37.

"The New Waugh," London *Times Literary Supplement* (Oct. 27, 1961), p. 770.

Nott, Kathleen. *The Emperor's Clothes.* Bloomington: Indiana University Press, 1958.

O'Donnell, Donat (Conor Cruise O'Brien). *Maria Cross: Imaginative Patterns in a Group of Modern Catholic Writers.* New York: Oxford University Press, 1952.

O'Faolain, Sean. *The Vanishing Hero.* London: Eyre & Spottiswoode, 1956.

Praz, Mario. *The Hero in Eclipse in Victorian Fiction.* Oxford: Oxford University Press, 1956.

Priestley, J. B. "What Was Wrong With Pinfold?" *New Statesman and Nation* (Aug. 31, 1957), p. 244.

Pritchett, V. S. "Cleverest English Novelist Alive," *New Statesman and Nation* (May 7, 1949), p. 473.

Rolo, Charles J. "Evelyn Waugh: The Best and the Worst," *Atlantic Monthly,* CXCIV (October, 1954), 80-86.

Savage, D. S. "The Innocence of Evelyn Waugh," *Focus Four,* ed. B. Rajan. London: Dennis Dobson Ltd., 1947, pp. 34-46.

Spender, Stephen. *The Creative Element: A Study of Vision, Despair and Orthodoxy Among Some Modern Writers.* New York: The British Book Center, 1954.

Stopp, Frederic J. *Evelyn Waugh: Portrait of an Artist.* London: Chapman & Hall, 1958.

Temple, Philip. "Some Sidelights on Evelyn Waugh," *America* (April 27, 1946), pp. 75-76.

Thompson, Alan R. *The Dry Mock.* Berkeley and Los Angeles: University of California Press, 1948.

Wagner, Geoffry. *Wyndham Lewis: A Portrait of the Artist as Enemy.* London: Routledge & Kegan Paul, 1957.

Ward, Maisie. *Gilbert Keith Chesterton.* New York: Sheed & Ward, 1943.

Watts, Harold H. *Ezra Pound and the Cantos.* London: Routledge & Kegan Paul, 1951.

Wilson, Edmund. *Classics and Commercials.* New York: Farrar, Strauss & Co., 1950.

Worcester, David. *The Art of Satire.* Cambridge, Mass.: Harvard University Press, 1950.

III. A CHECK LIST OF RECENT CRITICISM

Benedict, Stewart H. "The Candide Figure in the Novels of Evelyn Waugh," *Papers of the Michigan Academy of Sciences, Arts, and Letters,* XLVIII (1963), 685-89. Waugh used the Candide figure well in the early novels, but his later conservatism is "dyspeptic."

Bergonzi, Bernard. "Evelyn Waugh's Gentlemen," *Critical Quarterly,* V (Spring, 1963), 23-36. The clash between myth and three-dimensional reality, typical of Waugh, comes to its conclusion in the Crouchback novels, which may represent the novelist's "reluctant surrender to the modern world."

Carr, Patricia. "Evelyn Waugh: Sanity and Catholicism," *Studies,* L (Autumn, 1962), 388-99. Hails Waugh's emergence from a sense of the aimlessness of the modern age to a belief in Catholicism as a coherent vision of life.

Doyle, Paul A. "The Politics of Evelyn Waugh," *Renascence,* XI (Summer, 1959), 171-75. The novels do not propagandize for religion or class.

Dyson, A. E. "Evelyn Waugh and the Mysteriously Disappearing Hero," *Critical Quarterly,* II (Spring, 1960), 72-79. Although the range of his sympathy is narrow, Waugh's achievement is considerable, particularly his realistic representation of sophisticated "worthlessness."

Feinberg, Leonard. *The Satirist: His Temperament, Motivation and Influence.* Ames: Iowa State University Press, 1963. References to Waugh throughout this survey seem to rest on the assumption that he is no moralist, that he is negative and destructive, revealing hatred of the "modern" rather than Christian love.

Green, Peter. "Du Côté de chez Waugh," *Review of English Literature* (Leeds), II (April, 1961), 89-100. *A Handful of Dust* is Waugh's one flawless work; in it the writer has perfectly balanced "romance, satire, religious feeling, moral anger, wit, irony."

Greenblatt, Stephen Jay. *Three Modern Satirists: Waugh, Orwell, and Huxley* (Yale College Series.) New Haven, Conn.: Yale University Press, 1965. These three regard modern man as "caught up in a horrid circle of dehumanization."

Greene, George. "Scapegoat with Style: The Status of Evelyn Waugh," *Queens Quarterly*, LXXI (Winter, 1965), 485-93. A perceptive appreciation of the "conscious elegance" of Waugh's later style.

Hall, James. "Stylized Rebellion: Evelyn Waugh," *The Tragic Comedians.* Bloomington: Indiana University Press, 1963, pp. 45-65. Waugh's characteristic early theme was the power of "stylized rebellion" to shape the lives of even those characters too sensitive or too hostile to live by its code.

Hardy, John Edward. *"Brideshead Revisited:* God, Man, and Others," *Man in the Modern Novel.* Seattle: University of Washington Press, 1964, pp. 159-74. The failure of *Brideshead* is a formal one; it results from a clash between satire and "romance."

Highet, Gilbert. *The Anatomy of Satire.* Princeton, N.J.: Princeton University Press, 1962. A number of allusions relate Waugh to the satiric tradition and to particular satiric modes. Good on the personal element in the satires.

Hines, Leo. "Waugh and His Critics," *Commonweal* (April 13, 1962), pp. 60-63. A defender points out that Waugh has satirized his aristocrats as well as "the lower orders."

Isaacs, Neil D. "Evelyn Waugh's Restoration Jesuit," *Satire Newsletter,* II (Spring, 1965), 91-94. Parallels between Waugh's Father Rothschild S. J. and Thackeray's Father Holt S. J. (*Henry Esmond*) indicate that Waugh's priest is a "satire of the type-characters of historical fiction."

Jebb, Julian. "Evelyn Waugh: An Interview," *Paris Review,* VIII (Summer-Fall, 1963), 73-85. Waugh, a thorny subject for his interviewer, is terse, opinionated, and likable in this dialogue; but the man remains concealed behind his wit.

Kermode, Frank. "Mr. Waugh's Cities," *Puzzles and Epiphanies.* London: Routledge & Kegan Paul, 1962, pp. 164-75. *Brideshead* is found, once again, to reveal Waugh's "historical intransigence" more explicitly and less successfully than *A Handful of Dust,* "one of the most distinguished novels of the century."

Kernan, Alvin. "The Wall and the Jungle: The Early Novels of Evelyn Waugh," *Yale Review,* LIII (Winter, 1963), 199-220. The conflict between order and barbarism underlies Waugh's early novels; arrangement of parts and incidents establishes the "meaning."

Kleine, Don W. "The Cosmic Comedies of Evelyn Waugh," *South Atlantic Quarterly,* LXI (April, 1962), 533-39. Waugh's real subject is the "quest for value in the modern world"; the early novels are narrow but perfect achievements.

La France, Marston. "Context and Structure in Evelyn Waugh's *Brideshead Revisited,*" *Twentieth Century Literature,* X (April, 1964), 12-18. *Brideshead* is not really dissimilar to the early novels; in fact, the best of the work belongs with the early novels, the rest being "empty rhetoric."

Lapicque, F. "La Satire Dans L'Oevre D'Evelyn Waugh," *Etudes Anglaises,* X (Juilett-Septembre, 1957), 193-215. Tracing the conflict between "les modernes" and "les anciens" through Waugh's novels, Lapicque regards *Brideshead* as a single exception to "un humanisme . . . presque universelle," and concludes, of the central characters, that "c'est la pureté et la ferveur de leur effort pour calmer la détress morale . . . de leur âge" that creates "la grandeur de la pensée satirique d'Evelyn Waugh."

McCormick, John. "Allegory and Satire," *Catastrophe and Imagination.* London, New York, Toronto: Longmans, Green & Co., 1957, pp. 268-301. Waugh and the English satiric tradition stemming from Firbank are treated without appreciation or sympathy. All the stock criticisms of Waugh's later career are repeated.

Marcus, Stephen. "Evelyn Waugh and the Art of Entertainment," *Partisan Review,* XXIII (Summer, 1956), 348-57. No satirist,

Waugh is a superior "entertainer." Unlike some American writers who have attempted more than they could achieve, he has accepted his own limitations.

Mikes, George. "Evelyn Waugh," *Eight Humorists.* London: Wingate, 1954, pp. 131-46. Mikes defends Waugh (with gusto) against all criticisms, though he regrets some trace of cruelty in the satirist's treatment of children.

Nichols, James W. "Romantic and Realistic: The Tone of Evelyn Waugh's Early Novels," *College English* (October, 1962), pp. 45-56. "The tension between Waugh's realistic appraisal of what the modern world is like and his romantic yearning for a system of values . . . informs the tone and provides the satiric standard of his early novels."

Stürzl, Erwin. "Evelyn Waughs Romanwerk: Makabre Farce oder 'Menschliche Komodie'?" *Die Neueren Sprachen,* VIII (1959), 314-26. Never were the methods of comparative literature more ponderously applied than in this essay which analyzes Waugh's satires in the light of Balzac's aims in *The Human Comedy.*

Voorhees, R. J. "Evelyn Waugh's War Novels," *Queens Quarterly,* LXV (Spring, 1958), 53-63. Although the first two volumes of the Crouchback trilogy are a tribute to the upper class and to Roman Catholicism, there is nothing irresponsible in the art of this satirist.

Wasson, Richard. "*A Handful of Dust:* Critique of Victorianism," *Modern Fiction Studies,* VII (1961-62), 327-37. The novel is seen as a thoroughgoing attack on Victorianism and its continuing influence.

IV. BIBLIOGRAPHIES

Doyle, Paul A. "Evelyn Waugh: A Bibliography," *The Bulletin of Bibliography,* XXII (1957), 57-62.

Linck, Charles E., Jr. "Works of Evelyn Waugh, 1910 to 1930," *Twentieth Century Literature,* X (April, 1964), 19-25.

Index